*The Personal Jesus*

R. Earl Allen

# The Personal Jesus

BROADMAN PRESS
Nashville, Tennessee

4282-22
ISBN: 0-8054-8222-9

*Library of Congress Catalog Card Number: 70-178053*
Dewey Decimal Classification: 232
Printed in the United States of America

*To the Congregation of*

---

*Rosen Heights Baptist Church*
*Fort Worth, Texas*
*because of childhood memories*
*and*
*fifteen years together as*
*pastor and people*

# Preface

When my personal library numbered less than a dozen books, *We Would See Jesus* by George Truett occupied a very prominent place. Nearly thirty years and 6,000 books later, it still does!

The devotional desire to see Jesus in his humanity and deity was awakened in me by this princely preacher. With the passing of years there has been an earnest desire to see our Lord and Savior more clearly. These devotionals were prepared for the people of Rosen Heights Baptist Church and the book is so dedicated.

I am deeply grateful to my valued friend and editor Bill Cannon, who "reads me," for encouraging me to prepare them for publication. Deep appreciation to Miss Arline Harris and Mrs. Alfred Brian, Jr. for their tireless efforts and assistance in seeing this manuscript through to completion.

Gratefully,
R. Earl Allen

# *Foreword*

Both the form and the pattern of these chapters has been determined by the purpose for which they were produced. The author has assembled one of the most productive "preaching libraries" in America. Not only this, but he uses it! He composes his messages with a delicate sense of accuracy and freshness. He does not waste words; preferring one to two, and is always searching for words easily heard and strongly remembered. He knows that one cannot shake a sermon out of his sleeve and so he works at it like an artist who hopes to share the vision of his soul on his canvas.

He is acutely aware of his role as pastor-preacher. His theology is sound and undergirds all he says. He is first and foremost a preacher of the Word who knows how to communicate with people of all levels. He is thoroughly capable of addressing himself, with thoroughness and effectiveness, to the theological implications of the deity of Jesus, and often does so.

He knows his congregation's needs as well as any pastor I know. I am not surprised, therefore, that he has sought to help them understand "that Jesus was man as well as God." The messages in this book are convincing. One feels almost as if the man, Christ Jesus, had walked into his life and spoken his "peace, be still" in each instance.

The author touches no subject without shedding light upon

it from the glowing mind and heart that characterize him. You will not find him repeating the commonplaces; he has researched his subject well and fills his messages with the unexpected. His fifteen-year stay in the pulpit of the church of his boyhood is a signal achievement. Sunday after Sunday he preaches to hundreds in one of the southwest's larger auditoriums. Day after day he maintains a pastoral schedule that would be totally wearying to the average man. Add to this a study discipline out of which has come eight books and you have the measure of the man.

Dr. John Watson once said, "I now clearly see that every sentence should suggest Christ, and every sermon, even though his name had not been mentioned, nor his words quoted, should leave the hearers at the feet of Christ."

Dr. Allen does that in this book!

Carl E. Bates
Pastor's Study
Charlotte, North Carolina

*Contents*

---

# *"Sir, We Would See Jesus!"*

*The same [Greeks] came, therefore, to Philip . . . and desired him, saying, Sir, we would see Jesus.*
(John 12:21)

# 1 *The Personal Jesus*

One Christmas season, in a children's hospital ward, visitors went from bed to bed passing out fruit. Most of the children, relishing the special treat in this charity hospital, ate theirs quickly. One small boy, whose family was far away, left his fruit uneaten. It lay for a long time on his pillow, until it nearly spoiled, and the hospital staff thought it was wasted. But to the little boy, it was not only food to eat but it meant that someone cared. He may have gotten more out of that fruit than any of the others. He saw something in the gift, and in the givers' faces, that no one else saw. He understood the real purpose with which they had come.

To know that someone cares—that is the heart-cry of almost everyone at some time in his life. The answer lies in knowing the personal Jesus.

Young people today, particularly, are questing for truth. "What is the real purpose of life?" they ask. But "Who am I?" and "Where am I going?" will never be answered until first we get down to basics and ask, "Who is God?" "Where is God?" and "What is God like?" When we know more about God, we can more easily discover what he is trying to say to each of us.

In our time, men are still incurably religious, whether they admit it or not. It is evidenced all over the world in new cults that emphasize mysticism, meditation, even superstition. It is impossible to tear out of the deep recesses of man's soul the desire to seek something or someone higher and better. All men quest for the preexistent one, although their efforts at worship differ a great deal and usually fall far short of reality.

The book of Job records the cry of man in distress: "Oh, that I knew where I might find him [God]!" (23:3). This cry has come from beds of pain and death and from loving hearts standing beside them. This cry has risen out of emergency situations of life and from men under deep conviction. When holy moments uplift the spirit, we cry, "Oh, that I might know him better!" When Job's prayer was answered, he exclaimed, "I have heard of thee by the hearing of the ear: but now mine eye seeth thee" (42:5).

Near the end of the three years of Jesus' ministry, certain Greeks came to his disciples, wanting to see the Master. There were long generations of Jewish history behind this incident. In the Old Testament, God's message had been almost exclusively to Israel, and Jesus had preached chiefly to the Jews. Evidently these unnamed Gentiles came hesitantly to the edge of the crowd and one tugged at the sleeve of the most sympathetic individual he could see. Philip was not in the inner circle but on the edge of the crowd, seeing that everybody was taken care of and things went well. The strangers recognized the sensitivity of his spirit.

"Sir," they said, "we would like to see Jesus." They had heard of Jesus' great miracles, especially the raising of Lazarus. Among the gods they knew, they had none like this man. "We want to see God," they pled.

To see God, you must know his Son. It is not enough to hear of salvation from others. It must become personal and real.

Why did they search for Jesus?

"I came down from heaven," Jesus said, and, "the living Father hath sent me" (John 6:38,57). He had come to reveal God, yet he called himself most often "the Son of man."

The Greeks recognized that Jesus was uniquely different.

John, the beloved apostle, reached into preexistence and brought God down into time, saying, "The Word was made flesh, and dwelt among us" (John 1:14).

Especially at Christmas, we use his name *Emmanuel*, "God with us." Jesus Christ was God *and* man. The only time when the hyphen is properly used between those two words is concerning Jesus. We may say, "God and man" or "God-comma-man," but Jesus was the *God-man.*

"Can any good come out of Nazareth?" some of his critics asked. Yes, Jesus did. He came to redeem and transform! These Greeks recognized something about the personality of Jesus that attracted them.

His life as a man was an example of righteousness. He spoke no false or idle words, harbored no thoughts of revenge. Jesus was magnetic. Some have called him the supreme egotist of the ages because he dared challenge his critics by saying, "I, if I be lifted up from the earth, will draw all men unto me!" (John 12:32). But "it behooved him to be made like unto his brethren, that he might be a merciful and faithful high priest" (Heb. 2:17).

The Greeks were attracted to Jesus because of his humanity. He was as much man as any individual, as human as though he were not God. Let us hasten to say that he was as much God as though he were never man. He became tired with travel and went to sleep in a tossing boat. If he had lived in a supernatural body, he would not have needed food and sleep. He was "the Son of man," but he was not Superman. His body could not turn away bullets, had there been bullets in that day. Nails pierced his hands, a sword pierced his side, thorns pierced his forehead. Thirst blistered his lips and great agony caused him to sweat blood. He had a body like ours and knew the frailties of flesh.

Critics try to minimize the human part of Jesus, to make him seem so different from us we cannot realize how he can identify with us. His contemporaries knew him as the son of Joseph, a carpenter.

He lived without sin, not because he could not sin, but, yielded to God's Spirit, he *would* not sin. There is a vast difference. He was tempted as we are, yet no one found him faulty. "Never man spoke like this man," the temple guards said of him when they returned to the chief priests and Pharisees without capturing him (John 7:46).

What was so different about him? Look at the hall of fame of the spiritual giants of God's Book. Job was noted for his patience. When disasters came, his wife advised him to curse God and die. "The Lord gave," he said, "and the Lord hath taken away; blessed be the name of the Lord" (Job 1:21). Yet when Jesus was reviled and spit upon, he was more patient than Job.

Moses was called "very meek, above all the men which were upon the face of the earth" (Num. 12:3). He spent much time in the presence of God and asked to see his face. But no man could look on God's face and live. He was given only a glimpse of his back. After that, Moses' face shone with such radiance he had to wear a veil over it for a long time (see Ex. 33–34)! Yet Jesus veiled his deity with humanity and became more meek than Moses, remaining silent even before the taunts of Herod.

Solomon's wisdom was famous. God appeared to Solomon in a vision and offered to grant a request. Humbly, Solomon asked for wisdom, and God was pleased, giving him riches and fame besides. But Jesus announced to the world that "a greater than Solomon is here" (Matt. 12:42).

The title of "the beloved apostle" was bestowed upon John, the son of Zebedee, but who taught him how to love? He and his brother James were once called "the sons of thunder" (Mark 3:17). Evidently John had a temper like a firecracker until love, in the person of Jesus, transformed his life.

No man was more zealous than the apostle Paul, yet the experience of meeting Jesus on the Damascus road changed him from being a persecutor to being persecuted. Jesus, all his earthly life, was the "Lamb of God" who "opened not his mouth." (See Isa. 53:7 and Acts 8:32.)

These were traits of Jesus' humanity, yet he was also the unchanging Christ, the Son of God. He was born of a virgin, of the seed of the Spirit of God. It was the only time a child has ever been born without an earthly father. In taking on himself the form of man, God invaded history. Jesus was "made flesh" at Bethlehem.

Death claimed Jesus, as it has claimed all other men, yet death was destroyed forever by that victim, who became its victor.

Jesus counted it both a duty and a delight to take upon himself the form of a man. He laid down his body, for "no man can take it from me," he said. "Father, into thy hands I commend my spirit," he cried on the cross (Luke 23:46). How dared mortal man lay hands on the immortal God? God created Adam by drawing dust together and breathing his life into it. In disobedience and depravity, the creature rose up to kill the Creator, taking God's Son in human flesh and crucifying him.

As the gospel song says, Jesus "could have called ten thousand angels." Gabriel would have blown his trumpet and called out all the guardians of heaven to rescue the Son—if God had permitted. Surely they stood close to the gates, ready to come down and impede the hammer, to snatch the nails, to destroy the destroyers—but God did not ordain it that way.

One thing God did ordain, and that was that his Son should be the world's Savior. "But we see Jesus," wrote the author of Hebrews, "who was made a little lower than the angels for the suffering of death, crowned with glory and honour; that he by the grace of God should taste death for every man" (Heb. 2:9).

How do we see him? Not with physical eyes, but by accepting God's Word about him. Luke had many things to say about the personal Jesus. Like Luke, we did not live with him here on earth, but one day we shall see him. We have to know him through the experience of becoming a Christian and allowing the Holy Spirit to teach us of him.

How shall we recognize him in heaven? By the splendor and radiance of his glory. But here we need to know him personally, to know the glory of his presence in our hearts. As the songwriter puts it:

> I have seen him; I have known him,
> 	And he deigns to walk with me.
> And the glory of His presence
> 	Will be mine eternally.

*For God, who commanded the light to shine out of darkness, hath shined in our hearts, to give the light of the knowledge of the glory of God in the face of Jesus Christ.* (2 Cor. 4:6)

# 2 The Face of Jesus

During World War I, in Manila Bay, some sailors were swabbing the deck of a ship. One of them pulled off his jacket and hung it over the rail. Somehow, it went overboard. The boy started to dive from the deck. An officer, sensing what he was about to do, ordered him to stop, but in spite of the command he went over the side. Diving two or three times, he finally brought up the jacket. Because he acted in disobedience of an order he was brought before Commodore Dewey.

"You disobeyed a direct order," the commodore said. "What do you have to say for yourself? You endangered not only your own life but others who might try to save you. Why did you do it?"

The lad, realizing for the first time the danger of a quick decision, replied, "Sir, my mother is dead, and in that jacket was the only picture I have of her."

How important, then, is the face of Jesus Christ! There is the whole gospel in his face—"the light of the knowledge of the glory of God." It is not so much his features that are important, but his character revealed.

Actually, we know nothing of his countenance. That remains hidden behind twenty centuries of time. There was no photography in his day. No sculptor took a passing fancy to this humble young man. They saw nothing in him of immortality. They did not recognize at first glance that he was the King of kings. They did not sense that he would be more powerful than any military man, that he would have more knowledge than Solomon, that he would be a greater leader than Moses. They passed him by.

His disciples gave us some glimpses. They spoke of his eyes, his penetrating look. Peter always remembered the look of Jesus the morning after his trial, when Peter had denied him. The gospel writers mentioned his bearing and his attitude toward people who came to him but didn't attempt to picture his face. We are told to walk by faith, not by what we see, depending on no image, no picture. The paintings and sculpture we have are only artists' conceptions. We cannot find him in art galleries. The Holy Spirit alone paints the perfect picture.

What kind of mental image do you have of God? Some people think of God somewhat like Santa Claus. When troubles, trials, and sorrows crush them, their faith is shattered; they turn away from God, complaining, "Where was God when I needed him? He is not the God I thought!" Sometimes, even after we have known God, we walk so far from him for so long that we cannot quite recall what he really looks like.

Dr. John Brown of Edinburgh told of a minister whose wife died. He had no photograph, and he desperately wanted a picture of her. He could not commission an artist, even if he had the money, because he had nothing to show how she looked. Finally, he took some canvas and brushes and paints and shut himself away in the little study of his church for a few days. This man who had never painted before in his life brought out an amazing likeness of his wife painted from memory, out of the love in his heart. The image we paint with our hearts is far better than a brush picture.

Humanly speaking, what can we say about Jesus' face? Neither brush nor words could express what I would like to reveal. In the Bible we find some clues in what he was, what he did, and what he said.

Surely he had a delightful face. Some find nothing attractive, nothing glad, nothing cheerful about the face of Jesus. Isaiah prophesied that he would be "a man of sorrows, and acquainted with grief" (53:3). Of course, he bore our sins, and these have brought grief into our own lives, also. But God does not mean for us always to stay in sorrow. One man wrote that although Jesus was much under fifty years of age, probably his tears and sorrows made him seem older than that.

Some act as if he should only be thought of among the tears and difficulties of life. We often sing,

> I need Thee, O I need Thee;
> Every hour I need Thee!

But when? Usually, when tears are flowing and emotions choke our words until we can scarcely sing it. We need him then, but we need him at all other times, also.

There must have been an inner light in his face, a glory of spirit. Three glories have been differentiated. One is superficial or artificial. This kind of thing men can create, paint, change by cosmetic or design, by light or effect. Another is natural glory, where a person has vitality, personality, magnetism. A word much in vogue today is "charisma." Then there is an inner spiritual glory that Jesus certainly had, and God desires us all to have. The Scriptures say that "for the joy that was set before him," he endured the cross (Heb. 12:2).

The Gospels show Jesus to be the kind of person you would like to have at your dinner table. There was about him the kind of laughter that would make food taste better and digestion easier. Mary, Martha, and Lazarus were delighted to have him at their house, not because of his personage altogether, but because of his personality. They delighted to be in his presence. He was a welcome guest at weddings and banquets—wherever there was laughter. He was, indeed, "a man for all seasons."

That children loved him reveals something about him that his disciples scarcely understood. Children were delighted to be with him. They gathered around him, listened to his stories, perhaps clambered over his lap and reached up to touch his face.

He was not soft or effeminate, however. He had a dauntless and determined face: "he set his face steadfastly toward Jerusalem," the Bible says, fully aware that the road led to Gethsemane and Golgotha. "If you are going," his disciples said, "let us go and die with you." They tried to get him not to go. They did not understand his final mission and the fact that he must die.

During the Civil War, a farmer drove his wagon through his own army lines and then through enemy lines, trying to reach a surgeon in another city. They stopped him and asked why he dared such a thing. The man turned back some quilts in the wagon and revealed a sobbing, suffering boy. That was why he was willing to go through difficulty and danger. If you want to know why Jesus went to Calvary, go and look at yourself in a mirror. Nobody ever cared for you like Jesus, and Calvary proves it. He would not be hindered or distracted from the set course of the cup and the cross.

"I lay down my life," Jesus said. "No man taketh it from me, but I lay it down of myself" (John 10:17–18). All of Satan's temptations in the wilderness did not turn him from his Father's will. He went steadfastly through the suffering and death that would save the world.

He also had a face that was despised by many. This is a side of his profile we do not wish to contemplate often. The rulers of the Jews and many people of his day despised him. The world is filled today with despisers. As Christians, we will always have to pay something for our faith. Worldly people feel a little uncomfortable around somebody that is serenely and completely committed to God. They despised Jesus for the same reason. He did no wrong, but they hunted out a pretext with which to accuse him of treason.

In the same way the two thieves looked at him on Calvary, people today look at Jesus with either contempt or acceptance. Some will fall in love with him and say, "Oh, Son of God, have mercy on me." Some will look at him and turn away, cursing. The mob, the Pharisees, and the ungodly soldiers spit on his face and buffeted him. Mary Magdalene looked into his forgiving face. So did Zacchaeus, and the repentant thief on the cross. They saw there a hope they had not dared to entertain.

His was a divine face, because the glory of God was revealed in him. There was a glow of mission about the Master. Those who hungered for a sight of God feasted on the face of Jesus. "He that hath seen me hath seen the Father," Jesus said (John 14:9), for "I and the Father are one" (John 10:30). The world is still looking for a glimpse of God. Rufus Jones tells of a child saying, "I want a God with a face!" We all do—and the face of God is Jesus Christ.

Do others see any tenderness, any gladness in our faces that make them want what we have? Do they see inward peace? "Peace I leave with you," he said, "my peace I give unto you" (John 14:27). Do they sense the glow of mission? Don't lose the image of the glory of God in the face of Jesus Christ. Millions have painted his face with their lives of dedication.

It is said that during the French Revolution the Palace of Versailles was being ransacked by revolutionaries, and in the private chapel they found an artist's conception of the face of Christ. For a moment, they stepped back and stopped the plundering. Then one of them solved the situation by turning the picture to the wall. Immediately, they went back to their stealing and destruction.

Have you turned the face of Jesus to the wall? You know he can see right through you, and that may be anything but pleasant. Remember that he can also see in you something the world has never discovered about you, and they cannot, until they see in you the glory of God as you reveal the person of Jesus Christ. Wouldn't you like to be the person that God desires you to be?

His is the face that lights our way, for he is "the Light of the world." Looking into the face of Jesus by faith, spending time with him in prayer, changes us into his image, so that we also reflect the glory of God. As the ending of a song entitled "In the Secret of His Presence" says,

> And whene'er you leave the silence of that happy meeting place,
> You must mind and bear the image of the Master in your face.
>
> ELLEN LAKSHMI GOREH

*To Israel he saith, All day long I have stretched forth my hands unto a disobedient and gainsaying people.*
(Rom. 10:21)

# 3 The Hands of Jesus

The life of Jesus was many-sided, yet it would not be difficult to reconstruct it by describing the work of his hands. Even yet, there is still so much evidence of his life in the history of the world, so much of his personality revealed in God's word, so much of God expressed in song and service in Christ's name, that every one should get a glimpse of what being a follower of Christ really means.

If your assignment were to paint a portrait of the life of Jesus, how would you start? If you met someone desperately hungering after God, who said, "Tell me about Jesus; tell me the old, old story of his goodness, his mercy, his love!"—what would you say?

There are many things that we could say about Jesus, although time and the inadequacy of words limit us. We could say, in great rejoicing, that he is the best friend we ever have. He is everything the Bible said he would be and everything that God promised.

As we look at Jesus, more than anything else I think it is easiest to speak of the hands of Christ. We recognize in the work of his hands, and in their nail prints, the complete gospel. We come to know something concerning the great heart, the great mind, and the great sacrifice of our wondrous Savior.

Perhaps more has been said concerning the hands of Christ

than any other portion of his physical body. All of us recognize that hands have a language of their own. There is a sign language of the deaf. The Indian tribes used a sign language to communicate with each other. Yet beyond sign language, hands are often very revealing. Impressions come to us immediately as we grip hands with someone. There is the token of friendship and fellowship offered in the extended hand. Often we form an idea of an individual as we react to the grip of the hand.

Hands can save, soothe, or destroy life. The inner heart is revealed by hands that softly touch a fevered brow or rearrange a pillow in a sickroom. In the Bible, the phrase "the work of our hands" is very expressive (see Ps. 90:17 and other references).

We are told that our hands, besides our grip and gestures, are distinctively our own. There is no other quite like ours in all the earth—our handprint, as well as our fingerprints, is unique. There is also a special identity in the hands of Christ that makes him above and beyond all others that we could know.

A Mohammedan could take us yonder to Mecca—to the rock, to the place where Mohammed was born, and to where he is buried. But a Christian can go to the place where Jesus was born and to the place where Christ *was* buried—but he is not there, he is risen. We can only tell you about the nail prints in his hands and feet and the spear wound in his side that caused his death—but he arose from the dead.

What about the hands of God? The songwriter assures us that "He has the whole world in his hand." Sometimes we are tempted to wonder if God still has this old world in his hands—does any portion of it belong to him? Isaiah declared that "the Lord's hand is not shortened that it cannot save" (59:1). When God drove the cross into this earth of ours, it was more than a conqueror saying, "In the name of my king, I claim this continent." When God sent Jesus Christ, the planting of the cross was God's claim over a lost world that had alienated itself from God and gone its own way.

The hands of Jesus were, first, creative hands. In the very beginning of Genesis the word for "God" is plural, implying the Trinity. The hands of the triune God shaped the heavens and the earth, separated darkness and light, divided land and sea. The Bible says that after God made all things, he looked at it and declared it was perfect and pleasing in his sight. That was before the ugly snake of sin crawled up and down the valleys, across the hills, and stung the hearts and minds of men to death, and now the heart of man is desperately wicked. Even that which was beautiful in the sight of God has become spoiled with the stain of man's sin.

God made man and shaped him, as a glass blower according to pattern twirls and shapes, as a carpenter according to design saws and sands, as a sculptor molds according to his inspiration and mental image. With a heart of love, God shaped man in his own image. We are "fearfully and wonderfully made," said the psalmist (139:14). This ought to give man great dignity, the realization that we are the product of the mind of God and are left here to do the work of God. He breathed into man his own breath. We are living on borrowed time, using borrowed oxygen—we have nothing more than the breath of God. And when God says, "Enough!" a man has no more life.

It is not so much what the Lord was able to do with the dust of the earth, but the thing that brings joy to our hearts is the realization that after man blighted himself, God was able to pick up the remnants, and with the pieces make a new creature in Christ Jesus.

Near Walla Walla, Washington, is one of the first atomic energy commission units. A large area there was set aside by the government for atomic experiments in which they could not use man. They made a robot and sent it out under remote control to do certain things. Unexpectedly, the robot stumbled and fell, and could not get up. Unable to retrieve it, they had to make another one.

The robot was unable to raise itself. Neither can man raise himself! All men are as desperately and definitely lost as any robot that stumbles and falls and can never get up. But the hand of God reaches down and picks men up out of their sin, forgives them through the shed blood of Jesus Christ, and makes us fit to stand before him. The psalmist, glorying in this thought, expressed it: "He brought me up also out of an horrible pit, out of the miry clay, and set my feet upon a rock, and established my goings" (40:2).

There is yet another glory beyond that. Mark said that Jesus' hands were strong hands, the hands of a toiler. "Is not this the carpenter's son?" they said of him (Matt. 13:55). As Simon, John, James, and others were mending nets, Jesus passed by and called to them, "Come after me, and I will make you to become fishers of men" (Mark 1:17).

In Old Testament times, men called of God often made excuses. "Our tongues get twisted," they said. "We'll make mistakes; we are unlearned men." Moses said, "I am slow of speech" (Ex. 4:10). But Jesus told his disciples, "ye shall be brought before governors and kings for my sake, . . . take no thought how or what ye shall speak: for it shall be given you" (Matt. 10:18–19). As Paul stood before King Agrippa, after Christ's resurrection, the convicting power of the Spirit of God so moved that king's heart that he said, "Almost thou persuadest me to be a Christian" (Acts 26:28).

Christ's hands were healing hands. He was always sympathetic: teaching, healing, ministering. The tender touch of his hands was the talk of the whole countryside. There are three major professions as we know them: medicine, law, and the ministry. The lawyer is judged by the ethics of his conduct before the court. The doctor takes his Hippocratic oath, and there are ethics to be followed in his practice of medicine. But Jesus went everywhere, serving as judge, healer, teacher sent from God. Whatever the hurt was, the compassionate Master touched it.

Sometimes we long for Christ's power of healing—we cannot fully understand, we cannot manage to touch, we cannot seem to help. Only in the spirit of Christ can each of us reach out, in our walk of life, and give witness for him.

Jesus "went about doing good" (Acts 10:38). He touched the ears of those who were deaf, and they were able to hear. He touched the eyes of some who were not able to see, and they saw Jesus. They were able to see in reality for the first time. Then many came to Jesus who had leprosy—those who were banished from the mainstream of society. They did not have hospitals, as we have today, and the desperate, separating nature of their disease harmed mind and spirit as well as the body. When the lepers heard that Jesus was coming by, they went out on a lonely road with weary desperation. They called out a plea of dying men, "Jesus, Master, have mercy on us!" Jesus heard and Jesus helped.

Only one came back to thank him. "But where are the nine?" he asked (Luke 17:17). Where were the many that he saved? Where are those he has touched, healed, and once the emergency was over, their need passed, went their own way?

In the Old Testament, God's hands were pictured as hands of blessing, outstretched and beckoning. "I have spread out my hands all the day unto a rebellious people," he said (Isa. 65:2). God had tolerated their indifference and excuses from time immemorial. But one day, he declared, he would shut his ears to their cries.

When the Son of God came to earth at Bethlehem, he was God's stretched-out hands of forgiveness. Out on the Mount of Olives, across the valley Kidron, the lights of the city can be seen below. Jesus looked down on that Holy City, the city of David, and lamented, "O Jerusalem, Jerusalem, . . . how often would I have gathered thy children together, even as a hen gathereth her chickens under her wings, and ye would not!" (Matt. 23:37). I wonder if, as he stands at heaven's balcony and sees the lights of our homes, and the lack of spiritual light in our hearts, he says something similar today!

"The guilt of sin is still on you," God declares, "not because I won't do anything about it, but because *you* won't do anything about it." He would have picked us up, forgiven our sin, washed away the hurt, smoothed and healed the bruises—"I would have brought you to myself as a hen gathers her little chicks—but you would not!" Christ's nail-scarred hands were proof of his purpose, his identity, and his deity.

We can only declare God to you; we cannot make you fall in love with him. He still holds out nail-scarred hands, as he did to Thomas, urging us to touch them and behold the evidence of his love that took him to the cross and his power that brought him out of the grave. The scars made a difference to Thomas. He fell at Jesus' feet and exclaimed, "My Lord and my God!" (John 20:28).

"Behold, I stand at the door and knock," Christ said in the last book of the Bible. "If *any* man hear my voice, and open the door, I will come in" (Rev. 3:20). What bars the door? Indifference? Or procrastination? He knocks still, offering blessing and fellowship. This is the promise of God himself. He who stands at the door is the greatest guest you could ever have.

But you may be distracted by the morning papers or your own preconceived plans. Over the many noises of life, the knock of God may go unheard or ignored. Yet, when you are alone, there will be that persistent, still voice. God is standing silently nearby, his hand uplifted to knock, if you will listen, his hands outstretched when you feel your need of him.

"I will come in and sup with him," Jesus said. He'll break bread with you. "I'll have fellowship with you, as a friend," he promised. He is the best friend of all to have!

There is great joy and assurance in knowing we are safe in his hands: "My sheep hear my voice," he said, "and they shall never perish, neither shall any man pluck them out of my hand" (John 10:28). "I bear in my body the marks of the Lord Jesus," wrote the apostle Paul. He was saying that he was branded as a Christian, the property of God. Our hands might slip, but the hands of Christ are eternally sure and steadfast. They are transforming hands.

"All day long I have stretched forth my hands unto a disobedient and gainsaying people" (Rom. 10:21). We are often "disobedient and gainsaying people," yet Jesus reaches out his hands and transforms us.

*And she had a sister called Mary, Which also sat at Jesus' feet, and heard his word.* (Luke 10:39)

# 4 The Feet of Jesus

It has been said of some Christians that they had "one foot in heaven"—and, presumbably, one foot on earth. Jesus was not like that. His eyes were clearly on heaven, but his feet were solidly on the ground.

Have you thought about the feet of Jesus? An Old Testament prophet said, "How beautiful upon the mountains are the feet of him that bringeth good tidings, that publisheth peace" (Isa. 52:7).

We read in John's Gospel that the risen Jesus returned to his disciples, one of whom had said, "Except I shall . . . put my finger into the print of the nails . . . I will not believe" (John 20:25). And Jesus "showed them his hands and his feet" (Luke 24:40).

There are times when we have literally thrown ourselves at the feet of Jesus in sorrow and anguish. In bowing before him, we anticipate the Bible prophecy which says that one day "at the name of Jesus every knee should bow" (Phil. 2:10). Jesus Christ will be ruler of heaven and earth. Psalm 8:6 says, speaking of the enemies of Jesus, "Thou [God] hast put all things under his feet."

How do we come to Jesus? We should come as worshipers, kneeling—an altogether appropriate posture for proud, self-confident mankind. We find it hard to realize that every breath we breathe is by the grace and mercy of God. We could not live if God did not permit us to do so.

At the feet of Jesus is the place for the learner. Martha, hurried and frustrated because of the things she felt ought to be done for their guests, complained about her sister. "Master, don't you care anything about my problems?" she asked, in effect. "Mary is sitting at your feet, hanging on every word you speak, and here I am cooking and getting no help!" Martha's attitude seems very familiar: We want to tell each other how to serve God, rather than letting the other person use his own talents as God leads him.

Jesus was a guest in the home, and he knew what Martha was doing for his physical comfort—and that it was necessary. In answering, he indicated a special sense of values, outlined a divine priority. "Mary hath chosen that good part, which shall not be taken away from her" (Luke 10:42).

In the New Testament church they murmured against the apostles who ministered God's word. Why? Because they had not also engaged in a ministry of waiting upon the people. That's an everlasting problem for ministers and Christian workers, a continuing conflict, whether you wait on the people or wait on God or both in God's good time. When you wait on the people, you get what the people can give you. When you wait on God, you get what God has for you.

When Jesus' tomb had been sealed, his disciples thought he was gone from them, never to return, forgetting his promises. But when Peter and John went to the tomb that resurrection morning, they saw "two angels in white sitting, the one at the head, and the other at the feet, where Jesus' body had lain" (John 20:12). Angels wait at the feet of Jesus, serving submissively as his messengers.

There is an ancient hymn that says,

> 'Tis enough, my all in all,
> At thy dear feet to lie;
> Thou wilt not let me lower fall
> And none can higher fly.

Man on this earth will never stand any taller than when he submissively kneels at the feet of Jesus and asks God to reveal himself.

We are much like one of the disciples who, not understanding the Master's mission, but loving him, when Jesus said he must go to Jerusalem, Thomas said, "Let us also go, that we may die with him!" (John 11:16). Jesus has not asked us to die for him, but he has asked us to be "living sacrifices," our lives indwelt and used by his Spirit.

The footprints of Jesus show us a pattern. They made tracks across time that can never be erased. It would be well for us to look at the footprints of Jesus.

Scanty is our information concerning Jesus' early life, from the time of his infancy to the time of his baptism. Certainly it was always a path of submission. At the beginning of his ministry, Jesus took that path from Galilee to Jordan. He hasn't asked us to make any journey in which he has not preceded us and made the way for us. To John the Baptist Jesus said, "Thus it becometh us to fulfil all righteousness!" (Matt. 3:15). God's steps move in that direction, and so ought every Christian's steps.

The feet of Jesus moved in the paths of struggle, through defeat into victory. In these times, we have a way of justifying ourselves called "situation ethics," in which we say, "This is a circumstance into which no other person has ever been thrust. Surely reaction beyond the narrow letter of the law is permitted!" But the apostle Paul told the Corinthians that "There hath no temptation taken you but such as is common to man" (1 Cor. 10:13). Jesus was led out into the wilderness, and for forty days he wrestled there with Satan. The devil is very real! To forget that is dangerous!

At last, the Scriptures say, the devil led Jesus up "into an exceeding high mountain" (Matt. 4:8) to offer him rulership over all the earth. It is still true that the things the devil will show you will make you dizzy! He will make it difficult for you to keep your balance. But you can find the footprints of

Jesus all over the wilderness of temptation.

Jesus Christ went through the struggles without yielding to the devil, because he kept his eyes on God, thinking God's thoughts and quoting God's Word.

The footprints of Jesus led to service. His disciples didn't understand this. He said on one occasion that he "must needs go through Samaria" (John 4:4). Samaria represented a despised people they did not want to consider. We should not put on glasses tinted with prejudice lest we fail to see the needs of a world that is crying out to us.

It is well that we come into a church building and shut ourselves away from the world for a while that we might listen to the voice of God. But if we sit still very long, God is going to say something to us about following him elsewhere, because the feet of Jesus lead not only to worship but to service. "The Spirit of the Lord is upon me, because he hath anointed me to preach," he said (Luke 4:18). That is, to minister. Jesus is our example.

There is the path of steadfastness that he walked. He set his face "as flint" toward Jerusalem and the cross. When you have difficulty, what happens? Do you lose faith, quit church, confiscate the tithe? Do you question God? Or do you recognize that life has its tests, trials, struggles, but it also has its examples. Peter exhorted us to patience, saying that "Christ also suffered for us, leaving us an example, that ye should follow his steps" (1 Pet. 2:21).

Some of the words of the song "Footsteps of Jesus" say, "We will follow the steps of Jesus where'er they go." It is easy to sing those words, but it is a hard theology to practice. For the feet of Jesus got dirty in the dusty paths of Palestine.

It was a common practice for people to take off their sandals and bathe their feet when they went into a house. At a banquet, one sinful woman, out of love and devotion, opened a box of perfume "And stood at his feet behind him weeping, and began to wash his feet with tears, and did wipe them with the hairs of her head, and kissed his feet, and anointed them with the ointment" (Luke 7:38). This was rarely practiced even among the monarchs of the earth. To wash the feet was a meaningful thing, and this woman, who knew more about sin than she did about the Savior, mingled tears with the perfume and it was enough to wash his feet.

He walked a path of surrender: "Nevertheless, not my will, but thine, be done!" (Luke 22:42). In Gethsemane, he chided his disciples for going to sleep. The greatest danger of the church is not the sin and hypocrisy of its members, but the sleepiness and indifference of its people. While the Master prayed, while he interceded for a lost world, while he would lead us into the holy of holies of intercession, we sleep!

But in the steps of Jesus we find encouragement. It is a path of glory! The empty tomb was filled with the splendor of angels. They declared, as he ascended, "This same Jesus . . . shall so come in like manner as ye have seen him go into heaven" (Acts 1:11).

It is a glorious thing to be able to sit at the feet of Jesus. Martha prostrated herself at his feet when he finally came. "Lord, if thou hadst been here, my brother had not died!" she said (John 11:21). We come and throw ourselves before the Lord in times of great emotion, praying for the comfort of our souls. Why do we not constantly search out his example, follow his steps, and look for the clearly marked pathway of God?

On the Isle of Patmos, John had a vision of Jesus glorified, and described his feet as "like unto fine brass, as if they had burned in the furnace" (Rev. 1:15). "When I saw him," John continued, "I fell at his feet as dead. And he laid his right hand upon me, saying unto me, Fear not" (Rev. 1:17).

The path of his feet will not lead us astray. They may lead us into inner struggle, but never into sin. They may take you to a brookside of wrestling, like Jacob, that you might make up your mind whether you are going to take his best for you. If you choose "that good part," like Mary, no one can take it away from you! Sit at the feet of Jesus. Go into the Holy of holies and kneel before God, then walk out on the pathway Jesus trod—the holy path that leads to glory.

"And she had a sister called Mary, Which also sat at Jesus' feet, and heard his word" (Luke 10:39). Mary could literally sit at Jesus' feet and hear his word. Let us not fail to "sit at Jesus' feet" and hear his word.

*The friend of the bridegroom, which standeth and heareth him, rejoiceth greatly because of the bridegroom's voice.* (John 3:29)

# 5 The Voice of Jesus

Fingerprints have long been a method of identification, but there is now a new science of identifying a person by the unique electronic pattern of his voice. Now when young people ask each other if they are on the same wavelength, they are really saying a lot more than they thought they were. The voice has distinctive patterns just as personal, just as different, just as identifiable as fingerprints.

Strangely enough, our own voices sound peculiar to us. Do you remember being surprised the first time you heard a tape recording of your voice? "That doesn't sound like me!" we usually exclaim, often feeling shocked.

In this age of television, the video-tape is a marvelous thing. A picture of the person can be thrown across the nation, and even by satellite across the world. Several years ago I made my first video-tape, and I made the mistake of looking at myself present a brief message on television just before I preached. You never look quite that way to yourself; you find it hard to accept! And yet it is the voice and picture you present, faithfully reproduced.

What was the voice of Jesus like? We have written records of his words, but words and voice are not the same. Words are only part of the oral communication we make with our voice.

The Scriptures say that the words of Jesus are eternal and

everlasting. His words will never pass away. It also tells that his words were gentle. "Come unto me, all ye that labour and are heavy laden," he said, "and I will give you rest" (Matt. 11:28). His words were also words of judgment, for he said, "He that rejecteth me, and receiveth not my words, hath one [the Father] that judgeth him" (John 12:48).

Always they were divine words that fell from Jesus' lips. "The word which ye hear is not mine, but the Father's, which sent me," he said (John 14:24).

There were no tape recordings in Jesus' day, and there were no photographs. Everything we think we know about Jesus is the concept of some man, or based on some clue we find in the Word of God, as the Spirit gives us imagination. This cannot be completely decisive.

Adolph Hitler spoke harshly before groaning crowds of hundreds of thousands, with dramatic fire in the background, stirring a nation to war. Compare them to the oratorical words of Winston Churchill as, behind blacked-out windows, he said in a magnificent voice that had overcome stuttering in his earlier days—he spoke so distinctively: "Never have so many owed so much to so few!" and "This is our finest hour!"

What kind of voice did Jesus have? John described the voice of the glorified Christ, in the book of the Revelation, "as the sound of many waters" (1:15). Have you ever stood by a brook? A brook creates very little noise, slipping over the rocks smoothly, quietly, with a soft ripple. But have you stood by a waterfall? John said, "I heard his voice sound like one of the rushing waterfalls"—a powerful yet musical roar.

The voice of Jesus was not only musical but masterful. His words rang with confidence and victory. Word by word, sentence by sentence, idea by idea, the Bible portrays the voice of Jesus as an authoritative voice. Soldiers sent to arrest him returned empty-handed, saying, "Never man spoke like this man!" (John 7:46). They were not measuring his words, what he said, but the manner in which he spoke—the unquestioned authority of a master of men. "Heaven and earth shall pass away," he said, "but my words shall not pass away" (Mark 13:31). They were eternal and everlasting.

He had authority over the law. This the Jews did not fully comprehend, nor were they prepared for it. It was one of the reasons why they crucified him. They said he blasphemed. They wanted a gentle teacher who, without offending anybody, would rationalize and philosophize about their law. Some people consider religion only as literature and philosophy, and not as eternal truth revealed. It is one thing to come to consider religion as a philosophy, and it is quite another thing to face up to its demands as reality.

Jesus' contemporaries looked at him and marveled, "For he taught them as one having authority, and not as the scribes!" (Matt. 7:29).

"I am . . . the truth!" Jesus said (John 14:6), and his word still stands. That is not open for debate.

He had authority over the elements. One night, in a boat, Jesus peacefully fell asleep in a gathering storm, and it was not a feigned faith. The disciples recognized the power of the waves and the dangerous roar of the wind. Finally they spoke to him. They said the same thing we say when we get in trouble—as though it were God's design: "Dost thou not care that we perish?" Then Jesus "said unto the sea, Peace, be still" (Mark 4:39). Imagine, the power of one voice stopping the winds and the waves! "What manner of man is this!" they marveled (Luke 8:25).

What I thank God for is far more than that! He can control the elements—the winds and the waves, floods and tornados, blizzards and hurricanes—but he also has authority over man's sinful nature and over evil spirits.

In Mark 5 is an account of Jesus driving out evil spirits. Satan is a person; the devil is real. Today, in our nation, the worship of Satan is increasing. But Jesus drove the evil spirits out of men. When they were commanded to come out, we read, they pleaded that they might go into the hogs nearby.

And the evil spirits did to the hogs just what they will do to man. They stampeded them over a cliff (Mark 5:13)—off the deep end to self-destruction.

The winds and waves obeyed Jesus and the spirits were subject to him. God is still speaking in his authoritative voice. The problem is that few people listen. Our problem is not that God is dead or on leave, but that somehow we feel he is no longer in authority. When your faith fails, God cannot act.

We usually listen to people whom we respect—our families, and those whom we admire and imitate. But Jesus spoke with the authentic voice of truth, though it was questioned by many of his contemporaries.

It seems easy to listen to God's voice in church on Sunday mornings, when all is right with the world and the sun is shining through stained-glass windows. It is terribly difficult when cancer is wrecking the body or death destroys loved ones suddenly. Then we question Jesus' authenticity. We plead, like John the Baptist from a jail cell, "Go and ask if he is the one that should come, or do we look for another?" He was asking, "Is he the one from God? I don't mind dying here, if I am doing it for God. I just don't want to waste away in prison for nothing."

There are tests whereby we can detect whether a voice is of the spirit or of the flesh. Jesus spoke spiritual words. This was one of the acid tests of his voice. "The words that I speak unto you, they are spirit, and they are life" (John 6:63)—the authentic word of God.

We can be sure that it was the authentic word of God because in John 14, where he spoke of going away, but of sending the Holy Spirit, he said, "I will not leave you comfortless" (14:18). Later, he spoke of his Father's words: "The word which ye hear is not mine, but the Father's which sent me" (14:24). He had just spoken an authentic promise: "Ye believe in God, believe also in me!" (14:1).

The words of Jesus are lasting. Again he said, "My words

shall *not* pass away" (Mark 13:31). They were permanent. You can put them down and go back to them. You can pass them over, but you will go back to them. You can miss them, but you have to go back to them. The words of God endure forever. Jesus spoke with a voice that rang with the authenticity of God.

Then they were recognizable words that Jesus spoke. In the tenth chapter of John, he used that pastoral picture made familiar by David, yet added to its meaning. "My sheep hear my voice, and I know them, and they follow me. . . . My Father, who gave them to me, is greater than all; and no one is able to pluck them out of my Father's hand" (John 10: 27,29). The voice of the Son of God claimed that his own should recognize his voice.

Pilate, in a dilemma, asked Jesus to speak, and he remained quiet. He would not answer the false accusations. But when Pilate asked, "Art thou a king, then?" Jesus answered truthfully, "Thou sayest that I am a king. To this end was I born . . . that I should bear witness unto the truth." Pilate retorted—perhaps cynically—"What is truth?" (John 18:37–38). We do not need to question the authenticity of Jesus' words.

The prophets spoke, and their voices were stilled by death. The disciples spoke, but their voices became silent. The voice of the Son of God speaks forever.

Jesus had a patient voice. When John identified him in the first chapter of the Fourth Gospel, the Son of God, though he had taken human flesh as a baby and his voice was a small cry, came to mystify man and to magnify God: "the Word was made flesh, and dwelt among us" (John 1:14).

There were many centuries when the prophets no longer spoke, four hundred silent years between the Testaments, because God had no word for a disobedient people. Read the history of futility among God's people between the Old and New Testaments. Look at Malachi and think of the silent centuries before the magnificent words of Matthew began with the events leading to the coming of Jesus.

In the Temple, an old man saw the child in Mary's arms and said, "Lord, now lettest thou thy servant depart in peace"—he didn't even have to hear him speak. He was ready to die: "For mine eyes have seen thy salvation!" (Luke 2:29–30). There was instant recognition. The spirit of God bore evidence with his spirit that this was the anticipated one at last made flesh! The Messiah was proclaimed and identified by John the Baptist.

Some of the Jewish leaders said, "If thou be the Christ, tell us plainly!" (John 10:24). In other words, they demanded, "Do not mince words. Tell us plainly with an authentic voice. We have waited long enough!"

"I have come that they might have life," Jesus asserted, "and that they might have it more abundantly" (John 10:10).

His disciples had to wait until after his resurrection for their surety, however. A couple left Jerusalem after his crucifixion, going back to Emmaus. Their steps were slow, their feet heavy. Like you and me, they were disheartened, disbelieving, tied down to the things of this earth. "We hoped he was the Messiah!" they told the traveler who joined them. "We had waited, but we waited in vain." When the stranger broke bread and began to pray, they recognized his voice and his hands. Then they said, "Did not our heart burn within us, while he talked with us along the way?" (Luke 24:32).

The world waits for his voice. "Behold, I stand at the door and knock," said the risen, glorified Lord. "If any man hear my voice, and open the door, I will come in to him and will sup with him, and he with me" (Rev. 3:20). When his call comes in that holy urge, that quiet voice that will not be stilled, you can be sure it is the authentic voice of God.

The voice of Jesus is as the voice of a loving bridegroom. The voice of Jesus is always tender. The voice of Jesus is always gracious (see Luke 4:22). The voice of Jesus is always mighty (see Luke 4:32). He sends his Spirit to convict, to convince, and to prepare the way. He waits at the door of your heart.

I hear Thy welcome voice
    That calls me, Lord, to Thee,
For cleansing in Thy precious blood
    That flowed on Calvary.

'Tis Jesus calls me on
    To perfect faith and love,
To perfect hope and peace and trust
    For earth and heaven above.

LEWIS HARTOUGH

*For we have not an high priest which cannot be touched with the feeling of our infirmities; but was in all points tempted like as we are, yet without sin.*
(Hebrews 5:15)

# 6 The Temptations of Jesus

Paradise was lost in a garden, but regained in a wilderness. The Son of God, who had come down from heaven voluntarily, was confronted by Satan, who had been forced out of heaven. Jesus faced Satan on his territory: Satan had staked his claim on about everything in this world.

In the Old Testament, Satan spoke to Eve and posed the temptation that caused the first couple to disobey God. Satan challenged God concerning Job and raised the question, "Does Job fear God for nothing?" In the New Testament, he tempted Jesus—trying to get him to disobey God, as Adam and Eve did.

Some people consider Satan merely as an evil influence—those certain tendencies and weaknesses that are born in man, an evil that blows and bends the twig. According to the Bible, the devil, or Satan, is a person; we must recognize and take seriously this fact. We are told something of his purposes. What we do not understand, often, are his methods. The apostle Paul said, "Put on the whole armour of God, that ye may be able to stand against the wiles of the devil"—the methods of Satan (Eph. 6:11).

Some descriptive terms are used about him in the New Testament: he is vigilant, alert, everlastingly at his job. There is evidence today that he is very much on the prowl in this world. To him there is nothing sacred. Whatever Satan is able to grasp, distort, and ruin is his prey.

Satan's encounter with Jesus was awesome. It was a dramatic moment when they faced one another. Satan had subtly attacked the first man, the creation of God. He had accused Job to the face of God. In the wilderness of Jordan he finally faced the God-man. The Scriptures indicate that Satan was his usual self, at his best—or at his worst!

Certainly Jesus took Satan seriously. Many people speak lightly of him, or joke over things that are said about him. This is one of his subtle tricks. If he can make us laugh at him, then we will shrug away his insidious wiles and feel that he is not worth worrying about, that he is not really dangerous.

Jesus had no "worse," thus he was tempted at his best. People often take the attitude that temptation is always a very base thing. If that is true, we cannot understand how Jesus could be faced with it. There are sins of the spirit and there are sins of the flesh. Many have experienced meeting the temptations of the flesh. Many others have met temptations of the spirit. But we are not always aware that Satan is the author of some of the things we feel and some of the things we think and some of the things we say. Not every test is a temptation, but every temptation is a test.

Science tests and experiments with its theories and new discoveries. Industry maintains laboratories for testing its products. Cast steel is put under stress to see if it will stand up to certain jobs. Therefore the problem of temptation is not always moral sin. It can be a matter of testing, of adjusting to the pressures and stresses of life.

The encounter in the wilderness was not just a drama between Jesus and Satan. It was not that Jesus was unable to sin, for that would make him not human. But he was able *not* to sin. How can we explain the God-man? The concept baffles us. How can we explain that God could live in human flesh? There has been only one miracle of this nature—Jesus Christ, the virgin-born Son of God.

Immediately following Jesus' baptism, after he had been

identified publicly by John the Baptist as being "the Lamb of God which taketh away the sin of the world" (John 1: 29)—at that very moment the devil began to attack. Often a young person will say to a pastor or counselor, "Why is it that as soon as I get on the beam, as soon as I consecrate my life to Jesus, I have a harder time than ever?" This will always be so!

It has been said that "Consecration calls for choice, and choice initiates conflict." Until you make a choice, there is no conflict. Until you decide to walk out and out for God, until you consecrate yourself to the will of God, until you allow God to set you apart for his service, there is no division of interest, no antagonism between the flesh and the spirit. But when you choose to do the will of God, you have identified yourself as Satan's enemy.

In the time of Daniel, three of his Hebrew friends in Babylon purposed in their hearts they would not worship the king's image. These resolute young men were put into the fiery furnace, and the angry king "commanded that they should heat the furnace seven times more than it was wont to be heated" (Dan. 3:19). We live in an alien world and it will always give us a hard time when we serve the Lord.

After the descent of the dove upon Jesus came the attack of the devil; after the blessing, always the battle. This great forty-day period after Jesus' baptism was the first combat zone of his ministry.

The Scriptures mention that Jesus was "led into the wilderness." He did not fall into temptation. He was not seeking temptation. He had yielded himself to the leadership of the Spirit of God. You do not need to hunt for temptation; you can be sure it will track you down.

Temptation is as near as thought and feeling; as close as walking and breathing, as pervasive as sight and sound. Temptation is a part of living. It may be in asphalt and cement jungles, in the midst of silk and satin, around light and glamorous entertainment—but temptation is always "in the wilderness," wherever the "wilderness" may be.

This temptation occurred at the outset of Jesus' ministry, and included every possible area of life. A great English preacher, J. H. Morrison, said there are three times each day when temptation is most apt to come: at the break of day, when the glow of morning is gone, and at evening when the day's failures weigh on us. In these periods, there is often a physical relationship between how we feel and how we react spiritually. In our lives, many times, when conflict comes, we first meet it physically.

Satan spoke to Jesus concerning the problem of food, on the level of personal need. We cannot deny the necessity of food. It is basic. Satan began with the physical circumstances under which the Master had lived for forty days. Do you know what it is to be hungry? How long have you gone without food?

John the Baptist pursued a survival course in the wilderness most of his life—he had been eating crickets! At a South Dakota Baptist encampment, there were servicemen nearby who were on a survival test. It was tempting for us to offer them food, but they had to subsist on what they were able to find and prepare for themselves.

Satan started where you begin physically with a starving man and said, "If thou be the Son of God, command that these stones be made bread" (Matt. 4:3). What was wrong with turning stones into bread? Later, Jesus took five little loaves and stretched them to feed over five thousand people—he had the power.

In thus tempting Jesus, Satan was questioning the providential care of God, as he did with Eve.

"Man shall not live by bread alone," Jesus replied, quoting from the Scriptures, "but by every word that proceedeth out of the mouth of God" (Matt. 4:4). To turn the stones into bread would have been submitting to the rule of physical appetite.

Temptation on the physical level usually is as far as any of us go. We are captured there, in the maze of "God, we want!" and "God, we need!" until the other temptations at higher levels we do not often recognize.

Satan tried another angle—the spiritual level. He carried Jesus up to the pinnacle of the Temple. *"If* thou be the Son of God," he began again, "cast thyself down; for it is written, He shall give his angels charge concerning thee; and in their hands they shall bear thee up, lest at any time thou shouldest dash thy foot against a stone" (Matt. 4:6). The psalmist had written, "he shall give his angels charge over thee. . . . They shall bear thee up in their hands, lest thou dash thy foot against a stone" (Ps. 91:11–12). Satan urged Jesus to cast himself down so that God would perform a miracle in the sight of a great multitude in saving him. It would have been to court fame by over-ambition.

"It is written again," Jesus answered, "Thou shalt not tempt the Lord thy God" (Matt. 4:7). This was from Deuteronomy 6:16, and meant that one should not dare God on his promises, as many in modern times say, "If there be a God, let him strike me dead!"

It is a strange thing to find the devil with a Bible under his arm and a text in his mouth. Each time Jesus turned back against him the same sword. For Satan was quoting half-truths, and this is a dangerous thing! All sorts of doctrines and isms have built themselves on half-truths, claiming promises out of context, as Satan did here.

Satan tempted him a third time. "All these things will I give thee, if thou wilt fall down and worship me" (Matt. 4:9). All the kingdoms of the world! That should be the fulfilment of everything one could want—and it had been promised to Jesus by the Father, that to him "every knee should bow."

"Get thee hence, Satan," Jesus replies, "for it is written, Thou shalt worship the Lord thy God, and him only shalt thou serve" (Matt. 4:10). For the Master had made a connection that Satan had not specified, that what you worship, that you serve.

Satan was appealing not only to Jesus' physical needs, his spiritual needs, but now his material needs, on the level of vocation and ambition. "Take a shortcut," he was saying. "I promise you this whole world—right now!" But what good is Satan's promise? You can tempt little men with little things; Satan tempts kings with kingdoms. He promised the same to Alexander the Great, to Hitler, to Mussolini—and they all believed him. It is easy to get drunk on the satisfactions of this world. Jesus did not succumb to the temptation to compromise.

Then Satan left him "for a season," according to Luke 4:13.

The kingdoms of this world are not our problem as Christians. Yet one of our greatest temptations, especially in our spiritual lives, in seeking the will of God, is to take a shortcut. Satan whispers, "Don't pay the price of patience, of devotion, of dedication! Why, you can get by with so much! God is merciful and will forgive. You do not have to wait; you do not have to serve; you do not have to pay the price in responsibility." We should be very careful, therefore, that we are not listening to Satan when we think we are clever in finding an easier way.

These are some of the things we can learn from the drama of Jesus meeting Satan in the wilderness. Jesus quoted the first commandment from Scripture—naming the sin. "Thou shalt worship *the Lord* . . ." He used the Bible. He resorted to prayer and was led by the Spirit. Then he took hold of the power of God and commanded, "Get thee behind me, Satan! Leave me alone!" Our word may not be better than the devil's, but God's is!

Jesus promised his people that if we would call on him he would answer. He also will help us to win over Satan. "There hath no temptation taken you but such as is common to man," we are told in 1 Corinthians 10:13. We usually feel that nobody else has ever been caught in this particular web of circumstances. But the apostle Paul went on to declare that our temptations are no different, but that "God is faithful, who will not suffer you to be tempted above that ye are able, but will, with the temptation, also make a way of escape, that ye may be able to bear it." Do you look for the "way of escape?"

You never know in what wilderness you will meet the tempter, under what commonplace or dramatic circumstances. Temptation demands eternal watchcare and consecration. If Satan departs "for a season," do not think for a moment that he is giving you more than a recess or a coffee-break. The battle goes on unceasingly. The greatest temptation may not be the temptation of the flesh, but the temptation of the spirit to neglect God. To reject God's plan, to do "as little as you can get by with"—that's what Satan offered Jesus, as if we could ever get something for nothing!

All Jesus' temptations were connected with the cross in some way. He needed to survive physically to get there. He could hasten it prematurely by calling attention to himself before he preached God's message, or he could take the shortcut to rulership that avoided the cross entirely—worshiping Satan. Jesus recognized there was no lasting crown for him except by the way of the cross! Neither is there for us.

*And when he had looked round about on them with anger, being grieved for the hardness of their hearts, he saith unto the man, Stretch forth thine hand.*
(Mark 3:5)

# 7 The Anger of Jesus

We speak much about the love of Jesus—and not enough can possibly be said! John 3:16, that "God so loved the world . . ." is the pivotal point of the gospel. It tells man about God's love for him. It tells man about his need. It tells man that Jesus died for him. It tells man how he can be saved. If you never knew but one Scripture verse, it ought to be that one.

As we come to know the love of Christ, we have to ask the paradoxical question, "Do all men gladly accept this wonderful provision of God?" No, some rebel!

What is the attitude of Jesus toward those who turn from his love and reject him? The love of Christ, though above all imagination, is not a full-grown presentation of him. Jesus without anger—perhaps in our terms, righteous indignation—is not a full-length, in-depth portrait, for anger is definitely a part of the character of God.

If you like biography, there is an interesting story in the life of Robert E. Lee, the great Confederate general. In that noble soldier's last days, there came to him a group of men who stood at attention before him, as he sat in a rocker on the porch. They asked if he would lend his name to something that he considered unethical. "Leave me immediately," General Lee replied angrily, "or I will break my crutch on you!"

In this man there was still the integrity of what he believed. If men can become indignant over injustice, how much more God! It is wrong to think of the Son of God only as "gentle Jesus, meek and mild." He is tender as a mother, but also terrible as lightning. We cannot go our own way, rejecting, rebelling, blaspheming, without reaction from God. If you feel you can go against the will of God without punishment, then you do not know the Bible. You do not know life. You do not even know yourself—much less know God. In the end, he will demand an accounting!

Through the ages, some of the great ministers have been known for particular messages. Perhaps the most profound and scholarly, the most far-reaching evangelistically, one that stirred revival in New England, was the message of Jonathan Edwards entitled, "Sinners in the Hands of an Angry God." The prophet Joel said that "the day of the Lord is great and very terrible; and who can abide it?" (2:11).

Was Jesus ever angry? "That's not my picture of Jesus!" you say. "That's not how I think of him!" Do you think of him correctly? It is difficult for words to give us the completeness of the Master's personality as he really was. He said of himself, "Think not that I am come to send peace on earth; . . . but a sword" (Matt. 10:34).

The Bible says Jesus was angry, being "grieved for the hardness of their hearts." Did he lose his temper momentarily, or did he slip out of character? Many think this seemed very unlike Jesus. No! Think deeper than that! There is no sinful emotion, only sinful uses of emotion. God has emotion, as he is a person. He thinks, he feels, he knows, he acts.

Wallace Hamilton said that "Jesus did not get along with everybody, and that is both a challenge and a comfort." On a college campus, a chapel speaker emphasized that, as Christians, we should get along with everybody. Afterwards, an old Bible professor laid his hand gently on the younger man's shoulder and said, "Friend, if Jesus never aroused anger in other people, will you please tell me how he got himself crucified?" (It is a question worth thinking about.)

You have to live for, and sometimes you have to die for the things that really count. An ancient proverb says you can tell the size of a man by the kind of enemies he makes.

Jesus' true credentials, that he was the Son of God, were shown in his miracles. One day in a synagogue, Jesus saw a man with a withered hand. He looked into the hearts of the people there and saw that they cared nothing for this man's infirmity—the hunger of his family, the raggedness of his children, the mental and physical suffering of the man himself.

The onlookers in the synagogue, especially the leaders of the Jews, expected Jesus to work a miracle. But they refused to accept it as proof that he was the Son of God. They just looked at Jesus and thought, "We hope we can catch him out!" They didn't care about the good he was going to do, about how wonderful it was that this man was whole and strong and useful again and his family would no longer suffer hardship.

"By what authority do you do this?" they demanded of Jesus.

People react more violently to authority if it is on the other side. "By what authority?" But you can't take credentials from God out of your pocket like a credit card or a character recommendation. You don't have anything with God's name on it, unless it's your Bible, and of course that was written down by men. The evidence has to be on the basis of action or miracle. You don't take credentials out and say, "I do this by the authority of God!"

Knowing something about the needs of people and the heart of God should teach us, instinctively, what Jesus would do. He would help an injured man regardless of what day it was. As he said, "The sabbath was made for man, and not man for the sabbath" (Mark 2:27).

There should have been great rejoicing that day, but instead, they criticized Jesus. "You didn't handle the procedure like we have been taught!" How could they rather have the man continue with a withered hand?

I appreciated a man who called me on the phone and said, "I work with so-and-so," calling his name. "I have been trying to witness to him, and I know that some of his family go to your church. More than likely, he would be more interested in going there than anywhere else. I don't think he would be interested in going to my church. I wanted you to know I've been talking with him, and maybe you can follow through."

The anger of Jesus was directed toward the cold, hard hearts of those who reacted so unkindly. They were stiff-necked, rebellious toward the love of God. The Bible says, "He, that being often reproved hardeneth his neck, shall suddenly be destroyed, and that without remedy" (Prov. 29:1). There is an old song which we rarely sing any more, but which we practice often in daily life: "I Shall Not Be Moved!"

Jesus was interested in helping the person; they were more interested in law and procedure. God help us when we get more interested in the procedure than we are in the principle!

Compromise? Never! Reconciliation? Always! Jesus had righteous indignation against some things. He was "grieved in heart"—what a description of anger! This is the kind of anger that hates the sin rather than the sinner. Without comprehending this, we can never understand the depth of his anguish and suffering.

Florence Nightingale changed some things because she got mad over the filth, the misery, and the unnecessary suffering that sick people were subjected to in the hospitals of her day. The world has been changed by people who stand up with controlled anger and genuine concern against abuses and injustices.

Jesus was angered at the insincerity of the Pharisees who said one thing and behaved another. He was angered by the spiritual ignorance of the people. He was angered by those who tried to get to heaven by some other way, for he called them thieves and robbers. He was angered by those who profaned God's Temple.

The beauty and holiness of the house of God was withered in Jesus' day. One of the first things he did—and again at the end of his earthly ministry—was setting it straight. "It is written," he thundered in God's Name, "My house shall be called the house of prayer; but ye have made it a den of thieves" (Matt. 21:13). The money-changing activity made it seem like anything but a house of prayer. There was no reverence, and the priests were exploiting the people. Many worshipers came from great distances and could not bring live offerings. In the Temple, the priests' servants sold imperfect animals at inflated prices, and charged too much for the Jewish coins that were the only ones acceptable in the Temple offerings. Jesus said it was robbery.

There has always been, and always will be, attempts to use the name of God, the house of God, and the work of God for secular gain. Jesus was most angered as he stood in the Temple—it is the one time in his life that he raised his hands against a man.

One accusation the Pharisees made against Jesus was true: "He stirreth up the people" (Luke 23:5). Oh, that he would stir us up today!

There are some things God hates, and we should hate, also. Have you ever taken your concordance and made a study of the things God hates? One thing that causes the anger of God is for his business to be done in a slothful manner. In other words, you use your talents in the marketplace of the world, and do your very best. But you have a chance to do something for God, and you sluff it off carelessly!

Then, God said he hates anyone who destroys the fellowship of God's work. Remember the picture of Jesus as he "made a scourge of small cords," and with this whip in his hand, "drove them all out of the temple, and the sheep, and the oxen; and poured out the changers' money, and overthrew the tables." He said, "Take these things from here; make not my Father's house an house of merchandise" (John 2:15–16).

I hasten to say that I think there were tears in Jesus' eyes. It was not pleasant to him to have to punish anyone; he was brokenhearted. But it was something that had to be done, and he did it—before he went out and died for those he chastised, and for all other sinners.

*Jesus wept. Then said the Jews, Behold, how he loved him!*
(John 11:35–36)

# 8 The Tears of Jesus

Three times we are told in the Bible that Jesus Christ wept. This makes him different from all founders of the religions of the world.

Stand in front of Buddha and say, "My child is sick and dying of fever." Buddha would not say, "Go thy way; thy son liveth!" (see John 4:46–53). Buddha remains expressionless. When you weep, he does not weep, for there is nothing alive to acknowledge your presence; he is just an idol. Look to all the other religions of the world and you will not find in their particular prophets any intimate identification with people. The tearful, the suffering, the brokenhearted bring no emotion at all in their eyes. Our God is different!

The Son of God, wanting to identify with the world that men might know how God is loving and concerned, came to live among us. He did not weep all the time he was on earth. There were times when he was angry. Surely there were times when joy lit up his face.

It is said that "the common people heard him gladly." Children followed him in throngs, and children do not often follow a weeping man. Often there must have been a smile about his lips, a twinkle in his eyes. There was a tender touch from his hand. People were able to see him, to touch him, and to be touched by him in return.

He did not always weep, but when the Son of God wept,

it should claim our attention. Why did he weep? I am not sure that he wept for the same reasons we do. The tears of Jesus take him out of the realm of theology, however, and place him beside us in our everyday life.

Jesus wept more over the living than the dead, while we weep more over the dead than over the living. If we wept more over the living, perhaps there would be fewer tears at their death—over being too late for apology, over incomplete tasks, bitter failure, and lack of love. Jesus wept for different reasons.

Once I shared with a young couple sitting across the desk from me the fact that marriage triples your joys, but doubles your troubles—because the one that sits in front of you will weep some day at the funeral of someone they love, and the other will weep, also. They will come to identify their feelings, to empathize.

Most of our tears are over ourselves—something we did or something we failed to do. It is said that Alexander wept because he had no more kingdoms to conquer. Jesus could not and would not weep for this because later it was said of him that he had "the keys of hell and of death" (Rev. 1:18). He conquered all that he came to conquer.

Jesus conquered death, the last enemy. He closed the doors of hell to those who would seek the doors of heaven. He did not die as one who had failed to live. He lived more in thirty-three years than any of us will ever live in a lifetime. Regardless of the amount of our years, we will always have things left undone. Jesus lived the only completed life that this world has ever known.

Jesus did not weep over personal sins, for he had none. We cannot really comprehend this, because most of our tears are shed over our sins, whether we admit it or not. Esau wept because he had sold his birthright, counting the satisfaction of his hunger more important than the calling of God. Cain wept because there was a mark on him, the mark of a murderer who had slain his brother.

Peter wept because he had promised the Lord so much and delivered so little. Pilate's hall would not have been big enough—all of us would have to stand with Peter and borrow his handkerchief, because we find ourselves in the same situation. "Though I should die with thee, yet will I not deny thee" he bragged (Matt. 26:35). Yet before the cock crowed, he did!

Not one tear did Jesus weep over himself because of sin, for he had no sins of his own.

He did not weep because of anything he had lost, or would lose. He was going to lose his life, but he did not weep about it. How do we approach death? We can only take the lessons from those who have gone before us. Because ours is a highly medicated society, I am not sure we know how we would face death. Jesus did not weep over a fortune or position lost. It looked like he had lost everything, but he had gained everything. He had the "well done!" of his Father, though he had the rebuke of mankind. He chose the best.

Why did Jesus Christ weep? He wept over individuals. The misery of one small child brings tears to the eyes of Jesus. He wept over Lazarus' death. He wept with Mary and Martha because they were his friends—because they were hurt, he felt the hurt. This was empathy; you feel as your friends feel. It was a real, a personal thing to him. He cried in compassion and sympathy—tears, but not wailing. In the same way, he weeps over the death of any of his brothers and sisters—past, present, or future. Anyone who is a child of God is a brother or sister of Jesus and a friend of his. Though we did not see his tears, as they were visible at Lazarus' tomb, he weeps with the unknown and the known suffering and sin of each of us.

Jesus wept over a lost city because of its spiritual blindness and inevitable judgment. If you have been to the Holy Land, you will remember there is a vantage point on the Mount of Olives where you can see Jerusalem spread before you. "And when he was come near," Luke wrote, "he beheld the city, and wept over it" (Luke 19:41). "O Jerusalem, Jerusalem!" he lamented, "how often would I have gathered thy children together, as a hen doth gather her brood under her wings, and ye would not" (Luke 13:34).

At Hollywood, California, the Baptist evangelism secretary took me one night to a spot in the Hollywood hills where there is one vacant lot in that fabulous place of brick and mortar. High above the canyon and valley, from that vantage point you can see the lights of much of the Los Angeles area—three million people. He poured out to me his frustration in trying to reach a city that did not want to be reached. By their locked doors and closed apartment buildings, they seemed to be saying, "Let us alone!"

In the moonlight I could see tears on the man's face. I turned away, knowing there are some moments too deep for sharing in words. I thought to myself, Lord, is this how you felt over Jerusalem? Is there any way that we can ever feel as deeply as he felt? Would we ever have tears of concern over a lost world's separation from God?

Harry Clark, superintendent of the Pacific Garden Mission in Chicago for many years, was not an eloquent preacher. He couldn't preach without weeping over sinners. Feeling that this was a mark of weakness, he prayed that the Lord would deliver him from this habit. Soon he found his preaching power gone, the men falling asleep on him. Then he prayed that the Lord would restore his tears, and he found his soul-winning power returned.

Our generation has a way of saying, "Tell it like it is!" Jesus wept because he *knew* what it was, and what it was going to be for most of the people of Jerusalem. Before long, God would punish them by allowing their city to be destroyed. Jesus wept over their rejection: "Jerusalem, I would save you, but you wouldn't have me!"

"He came unto his own, and his own received him not," wrote the apostle John (1:11). God weeps over each of us. Hebrews 5:7 says that Jesus, "in the days of his flesh . . .

offered up prayers and supplications with strong crying and tears." On the cross, he "cried with a loud voice, . . . My God, my God, why hast thou forsaken me?" (Matt. 27:46). It was the only time he cried for himself—and yet his suffering was for us.

If we have not lost our compassion and our involvement with the world, we too will weep sympathetically with his suffering and concern over those who reject him. Tears are not a weakness. God does not condemn tears, but promises his children that he "shall wipe away all tears from their eyes" (Rev. 21:4), and turn sorrow to rejoicing.

But there shall be many tears at the day of judgment, tears of dismay and despair from those who have rejected him. May our tears be the glad ones of victory, through the power he has given us to overcome in his name. "He that goeth forth and weepeth, bearing precious seed, shall doubtless come again with rejoicing, bringing his sheaves with him" (Ps. 126:6).

*And they that went before, and they that followed, cried, saying, Hosanna; Blessed is he that cometh in the name of the Lord.* (Mark 11:9)

# 9 The Dilemmas of Jesus

Have you ever been on the horns of a dilemma? In the dictionary you will find that the phrase "horns of a dilemma" has become such a common expression that actually these words are used under the definition of "dilemma." What is a dilemma? It is two opposing views that cannot be reconciled, making a perplexing or awkward situation. A conclusion on one side seems as justifiable as a conclusion on the other. This is the dilemma—which way? It necessitates a choice, usually between unpleasant alternatives.

We are talking about the Son of God *and* the Son of man, not the Son of God versus the Son of man, for he was the God-man. He came to reveal God, yet he identified himself most often as the Son of man.

Many things must have happened to Jesus between the ages of twelve and thirty-three, but the veil is pulled. When the time was right, having lived in obscurity, unknown to the world, Jesus came with his swift walk into the very center of religious attention.

John the Baptist was preaching "Repent ye: for the kingdom of heaven is at hand" (Matt. 3:2). His baptismal services at the Jordan were the talk of all Judea. "One mightier than I cometh," John insisted, "the latchet of whose shoes I am not worthy to unloose" (Luke 3:16).

Suddenly, standing before him was the very Son of God,

Jesus, asking to be baptized of him, John the Baptist.

Why did Jesus wish to be baptized? Was there any reason for him to repent? Not at all! Why, then? He set a vivid and indisputable example. To any who are timid, shy, or slow, Jesus in a positive manner set us an example of the public affirmation of faith which he desired (see Matt. 28:19).

That presents a paradox: the sinless one standing in the sinner's place. As he came from the baptismal waters, the heavens opened and God said, "This is my beloved Son, in whom I am well pleased" (Matt. 3:17).

Mark pictured Jesus going from this high and sacred hour into the wilderness, where he was tempted by the devil. Why? It seems, from our point of view, unnecessary that he should be subjected to the things that God was surely exempt from. But the Son of God, when he took upon himself the form of a man, was as subject to all the problems of this flesh as we are.

Much emphasis has been put on his deity, but few have drawn a very strong line under the human Jesus. Our dilemma comes with accepting him as a whole man, as well as a whole God. Accepting him as the Son of God, yes! But he was also a complete man, not just the form of a man. This is not so much a problem of theological belief as of personal awareness. Jesus was tempted as a real man. He suffered like a man, thirsted like a man, hungered like a man, yes. But tempted like a man? Yes, that, too! The Bible emphatically says that he "was in all points tempted as we are, yet without sin" (Heb. 4:15).

He was also tempted as God. The devil said to him, in effect, "Why go through all this when you, being God, are able to do miraculous things; you have supernatural powers, don't you?" (see Luke 4:1–13).

Jesus rebuffed Satan with Scripture quotations. It would have been child's play for Jesus to make bread out of the stones. He had the power. But if he had, when we face temptation we could say that he used a miracle we are unable to perform. Jesus quoted a text. We can do that. Jesus prayed. We can do that. Jesus didn't pull off any private little miracle in the wilderness. Rather, he met the devil as a man and subdued him with the same tools that are available to us.

Afterwards, for three years during his ministry, he encountered every problem, every burden, every sorrow, every hunger, every loneliness, everything that comes to man. He fought every sort of temptation and wrestled with every sort of problem.

There was another dilemma in the ministry of Jesus, a continuing one. People saw in this idealistic itinerant preacher a desire to help mankind. All rushed to him with their problems. Many wonderful people get lost in life, with their dreams misshaped because they allow people to use them and to push them into things. But Jesus stood out strongly in making his own decisions. One of the reasons he was popular among men was that he had power to heal them and to feed them. "This is of a truth that prophet that should come into the world," they said among themselves. He would be a leader that the people would follow, they thought. But Jesus "perceived that they would come and take him by force to make him a king," and he left them (John 6:15). So there came the dilemma of kingdoms—the earthly kingdom versus the heavenly kingdom.

It was no dilemma for Jesus. He knew which was lasting and eternal. But to the mind of man the question was, "Why can't we have both?" Jesus' contemporaries saw in him an opportunity to set them up a little kingdom here and now. But Jesus came into the world to die for lost mankind, individually. In the thorn prints across his forehead, through the nail holes in his hands, and the spear thrust in his side, every one of us bled on Calvary's tree. He came not to bring a holy war, but to offer God to the whole world, to each man, person by person.

He was not interested in the earthly throne they offered. They felt they were complimenting him, and he did not jest at their offer. He tried to lead them to the higher throne, the throne of God. All through Jesus' life he had to walk carefully, sidestepping traps from friends as well as foes, until the appointed time.

Then there came those who asked, "What are you going to do about money?" The answer of Jesus has become a classic, often-used saying: "Render, therefore, unto Caesar the things which are Caesar's; and unto God, the things that are God's" (Matt. 22:21). This was part of the dilemma of two worlds at one time. No supreme court at any time has ever nullified the verdict of the Supreme Judge of the Ages.

"Just one world at a time!" he says to us.

A man came to Jesus and said, "Master, speak to my brother, that he divide the inheritance with me" (Luke 12:13). Jesus' immediate response was, "Who made me a judge over you?" The man was trying to say, "Give me an edge," that is, "lean on my brother, won't you?" Many people ask a preacher to lean on somebody for them. If you are going to lean on somebody, don't lean on them in God's name, unless you are doing it for God's sake.

Jesus said, in effect, "I want to hear the other side." That other brother had a problem also; if one had a problem, the other had a problem! The man never quite understood why Jesus wasn't willing to execute eternal judgment in the temporal world—yet all the evidence will not be in until the end of time.

Then there was a dilemma of the crossroads.

"There are two roads from Jerusalem to Jericho," James Black wrote. "It is one road in two directions." You can go one direction or the other: one uphill, one downhill. Jesus could have gone home to the relative security of his family. In the other direction lay the road of toil and pain and death. He had to choose. Surely the mortal man said *live:* "Let this cup pass from me!" But the Son of God came to die: "Nevertheless, not my will, but thine, be done" (Luke 22:42).

The direction Jesus took was up to Jerusalem. His disciples, in dismay and absolutely without understanding, said, "Let us also go, that we may die with him" (John 11:16). They felt it was a very foolish thing for him to choose to die when he could go home in safety. All of us suffer misunderstanding from those who ought to know us best. Jesus well said that "A man's foes shall be they of his own household" (Matt. 10:36).

Friends also can be a dilemma. There was Judas. From the beginning, men have tried either to pawn Judas off on God, on himself, or on the devil. He is hard to categorize. In the upper room Jesus looked at him and said, "That thou doest, do quickly" (John 13:27), and the dilemma of Judas was solved by Jesus in tenderness.

That last week before his crucifixion, Jesus went to the Temple. It was supposed to be the place of God's presence, a place of prayer. When Jesus came into God's house, he found it desecrated by commerce, and he "cast out them that sold and bought in the temple" (Matt. 21:12). They ran over themselves trying to get out. This time we are not told that he had a whip; it was the conviction, the accusation, the realization in their hearts of violating God's law.

Always, the dilemma of Gethsemane! Why did Jesus, when Peter took out his sword and cut off one of the guard's ears, pick it up and put it back, healed? It was so much like him! Yet the man was among his persecutors. So much like Jesus—but much unlike the rest of us, most of the time!

Simon Peter hurt the heart of Jesus, also. He was quick to pledge his allegiance, brave with a sword in his hand, but cowardly and silent when it was really dangerous to admit that he was a disciple of the Nazarene.

There was the problem of Jesus' silence. Pilate strutted around like an appointee after an election, threatening, "Knowest thou not that I have power to crucify thee, and have power to release thee?" (John 19:10). Pilate didn't realize that the one standing in front of him truly had power over life and death! Jesus didn't answer the accusations brought against him, or Herod's jibes. Silence, sometimes, reveals the majesty of God. Only by silence can God answer the wrong-headed—he just lets them beat their heads against the wall until they are willing to listen.

Then there was the dilemma at Golgotha. As the song-writer phrased it, "He could have called ten thousand angels" to set him free. Yet the God-man, who had power to destroy them with a word, let himself be nailed to a tree. He only said, "Father, forgive them: for they know not what they do!" (Luke 23:34). "I lay down my life," he told his disciples earlier. "No man taketh it from me, but I lay it down of myself" (John 10:17). They had to understand that he was dying voluntarily.

There were many other dilemmas. But there was that last dilemma on the cross—the God-man dying for those who put him there. The Jews looked up at him and sneered, "He saved others; let him save himself," and "If thou be the King of the Jews, save thyself" (Luke 23:35,37).

"If thou be the Christ," said the unrepentant thief, "save thyself and us" (Luke 23:39). Was not the emphasis a human one: "save us!"

Thus Jesus died, the just for the unjust—and we don't write stories that way. We don't write history that way. We tend to write it as we want it to be. Jesus died, when he could have saved himself.

His life and death and resurrection face us with a dilemma. What are we going to do with Jesus, which is called the Christ?

*And when they had sung an hymn, they went out into the mount of Olives.* (Matthew 26:30)

# 10 *The Song of Jesus*

After the Passover meal and the institution of the Lord's Supper, what hymn did Jesus Christ and his disciples sing? Probably it was Psalm 118, often used as the doxology of the Passover meal.

O give thanks unto the Lord; for he is good:
  because his mercy endureth forever. . . .
I called upon the name of the Lord in distress:
  the Lord answered me, and set me in a large place.
The Lord is on my side; I will not fear:
  what can man do unto me? . . .
The Lord is my strength and song,
  and is become my salvation.
The voice of rejoicing and salvation is in the tabernacles of the righteous:
  the right hand of the Lord doeth valiantly. . . .
The stone which the builders refused
  is become the head stone of the corner.
This is the Lord's doing;
  it is marvellous in our eyes. . . .
Blessed be he that cometh in the name of the Lord:
  we have blessed you out of the house of the Lord.
God is the Lord, which hath shown us light:
  bind the sacrifice with cords, even unto the horns of the altar.
Thou art my God, and I will praise thee:

> thou art my God, I will exalt thee.
> O give thanks unto the Lord; for he is good:
> for his mercy endureth forever.

Someone has said, "Let me hear the songs a nation sings, and I shall tell you how the people think." Christianity is a singing religion. It is the only religion in the world that has anything to sing about; it is the only victorious religion.

In our churches, the children learn very early—usually by the time they are three or four years old—to sing

> Jesus loves me, this I know,
> For the Bible tells me so!

Most of the songs foreign religions use today are those that are copied from Christianity. One of our missionaries in China said they were amazed and heartbroken when they heard in a Buddhist temple an instructor teaching little Chinese children, "Buddha loves me, this I know!"

Children are easily influenced. One child was so impressed during the Christmas season about sharing with boys and girls who did not have enough food that not only did he bring food that Sunday, but every Sunday for weeks. If we teach children to sing, then in the sorrowing quietness of the night or in terror of soul, as men, they will be able to sing the songs of Zion.

Job, in the darkness of his soul, cried out, "Oh, that I knew where I might find God!" A little later, after he was assured that "God, my maker, . . . giveth songs in the night" (35:10), he could shout "I know that my redeemer liveth!"

In Exodus 15 Moses said, "I will sing unto the Lord, for he hath triumphed gloriously" (15:1). The psalmist struck a chord on his musical instrument and sang a song to his sheep, "The Lord is my shepherd; I shall not want. He maketh me to lie down in green pastures: he leadeth me beside the still waters. He restoreth my soul" (Ps. 23:1–3).

The psalms recorded in the Bible were the songs of people,

reflecting the devotions of their hearts. When Israel was carried away into captivity, one of the sweet singers wrote, "By the rivers of Babylon, . . . we wept. . . . We hanged our harps upon the willows. . . . How shall we sing the Lord's song in a strange land?" (Ps. 137:1–2,4).

In the darkest period of Jesus' life, he had his band of disciples about him for the Passover meal. The deserter had already gone out from them. Then it was, the Bible says, they sung a hymn.

Surely Jesus was their leader. Have you ever thought of Jesus singing? One who was as approachable as he would certainly have a singing heart. We have thought of him in many other ways, but nobody has ever captured the fact that he was the singing Christ. And why should he not be? He knew the glory of heaven. He knew the messianic promise that God has "brought me up also out of an horrible pit, out of the miry clay, and set my feet on a rock, and established my goings" (Ps. 40:2).

It was the last day of his life, the darkest day of their lives, yet Jesus taught his disciples to sing.

Although we have never had a portrait or statue of him, have you ever tried to reconstruct the image of Jesus and sense his personality? Peter never forgot his eyes, especially the sorrow in them "when the Lord turned and looked upon Peter," who had just denied him (Luke 22:61). Yet nobody ever told us whether they were brown eyes, blue eyes, or grey eyes.

We have been told about the hands of Jesus, yet they were never described. We know they were nail-scarred, but nobody ever said whether they were big hands or small hands. We are not sure whether he was tall, or slender. There are no portraits—except through the imagination of individual painters, and such portraits have varied from one extreme to the other.

Surely we have thought about Jesus as being a pleasant person. I am glad the emphasis has been, not on his physique, but on his spirit. The emphasis has not been upon the man-God, but rightly, on the God-man. The pleasant Jesus—oh, how pleasant he was!

Judaism wanted to label him the "peasant" Jesus. They said, "Is not this the carpenter's son?" (Matt. 13:55). When they heard of his unusual miracles, they said, "Isn't this the son of Mary? Isn't this just a peasant?" Then in scorn he was labeled "the Nazarene." "Can any good thing come out of Nazareth?" (John 1:46)—the woe-begotten place, the peasant people.

But Jesus was made in the image of God to reveal God to mankind. Little children came to him and he took them in his lap and blessed them. Look at the muscles of the face and remember that God made us in his own image. There are twenty muscles for frowning for each one needed to smile. God made it twenty times harder for us to be difficult as for us to be glad. Yet most of us like to do it the hard way. When Jesus smiled, people flocked to him.

A wedding ceremony was the great social affair of his time. And Jesus shared with his friends and enjoyed that hour (see John 2:1–11). People must have liked to have Jesus with them. We cannot criticize Mary, the sister of Lazarus, for sitting at the feet of Jesus. Would you want to leave him just to fix a meal? Jesus told Martha not to fuss at her. What Martha was doing was worthwhile, but "Mary hath chosen that good part, which shall not be taken away from her" (Luke 10:42). Later, Jesus stood with the sisters at the tomb of Lazarus, and wept in sympathy.

To his disciples Jesus promised, "I will never leave thee, nor forsake thee" (Heb. 13:5). Although he was going away, he said, "I will pray the Father, and he shall give you another Comforter, that he may be with you forever" (John 14:16).

Wherever there is great grief, there is the great God. When there is great sorrow, there is the great Savior. When there is great sin, there is a great forgiveness. Where there are great problems, there is great grace. Where there has been great trouble, there has been the triune God to stand beside us. He not only counts the hairs on our heads, but the tears from our eyes. Remember that every time a tear falls to the ground, a tear of the Lord's is mixed with ours. The splash has become a little larger because he weeps with us—the sympathetic Master.

Ours is the only faith that features songs of joy.

Two Chinese mothers watched a funeral procession, a missionary couple in a pagan land burying an only child. "Isn't it terrible," one woman said, "to have to bury their child so; their parents are not with them, and they are burying their baby in a strange land."

"Yes," the other replied, "But it's not so bad for them—they believe they will get their baby back!" Singing the songs of Zion makes life easier.

In Isaiah 53:3, a long while before Jesus ever walked the face of the earth and went to Calvary's cross, it was written that he should be "a man of sorrows, and acquainted with grief." And yet he was a singing Jesus.

The sympathy and sorrow of Jesus was all for us. When he wept over Jerusalem, he was not weeping because he had been turned down, he was weeping because his people had turned down their opportunity of grace. "Daughters of Jerusalem, weep not for me," he said, "but weep for yourselves, and for your children. For, behold, the days are coming, in which they shall say . . . to the mountains . . . and to the hills, Cover us" (Luke 23:28–30). There would come a time when they would wish there were a song they could sing.

Jesus was crucified by fearful and angry men. There was quite a parade to the cross. The soldiers pushed through the streets, leading him along. Many people chanted, "Crucify him! Crucify him!" And yet, facing that, he could sing! Why could he sing? He could sing because he was going voluntarily: "I lay down my life, that I might take it again" (John 10:17). He was singing because he was going home from a sinful, rejecting, despising world.

A historian has said that one of the greatest tragedies of our modern world, besides the sinking of the Titanic, was when a great textile mill in New England burned. More than a hundred young women were trapped and burned to death. Loved ones outside couldn't get to them, but they could hear them singing, as long as they were alive, "Nearer, My God, to Thee!"

Jesus sang. What did he sing? He sang the songs of Zion. He sang the songs of his people. What were they? The Psalms, especially the 116th, 117th, and 118th psalms were songs, and the 118th was often used as a doxology, as we sing, "Praise God from whom all blessings flow."

Jesus, leading his disciples out toward Gethsemane, must have sung the songs they knew from their early religious training. There was no other hymnal than the book of Psalms. They sang psalms they knew by memory, the words they had learned at their mothers' knees. "It is better to trust in the Lord than to put confidence in man" (Ps. 118:8) and "I will not fear what man can do unto me." It was a courageous song, a song of faith, a song of boldness. Can we sing that song?

Jesus had said that we have to come to him as a little child. Who dares to have as much faith as a child? He cries, and knows that somebody will take care of him. He calls, and knows that somebody will come to him. Who dares to have the faith of a child—to go to bed, like a child, and not worry about the morning?

We have to quit trying to be self-sufficient. We have to quit trying to do it ourselves. We have to trust him and say, "O Lord, here I am, and I turn my life—all of it—over to you." When you have done that, you can sing triumphantly the songs of faith.

In the Baptist Historical Society of Virginia there is a lock and key that came from a jail where Elder Waller and five young preachers were imprisoned for proclaiming the glorious gospel of Jesus Christ against the dictates of the State church. What did they do? Marched off to jail, heavily guarded, they couldn't preach, but Elder Waller said, "Let's sing!" And they sang. People followed them to the jail and gathered around to listen to their singing and their preaching.

Paul and Silas were put in chains in a Roman prison in Philippi. They had been severely flogged, but in spite of their painful backs, they sang in the night (Acts 16:25). Singing always makes the burden lighter. I don't know how well Paul could sing, but he surely could pray. And those songs and prayers shook heaven, and heaven shook the earth, and the door fell down, its locks broken. The jailer was impressed by that new song he heard that night—he was used to cursing and blaspheming. But these men praised God and sang songs in the night.

Those who are redeemed will be able to sing a new song, and to sing in the darkest night. The angels will fold their wings to listen to our song of redemption in heaven, where we will be able to sing in truth and in harmony,

> When we've been there ten thousand years,
> Bright shining as the sun,
> We've no less days to sing God's praise,
> Than when we first begun.

Do you have a song? If you belong to Jesus you should: "Wonderful, wonderful Jesus, in the heart he implanteth a song!"

*These words spoke Jesus, and lifted up his eyes to heaven, and said, Father, the hour is come; glorify thy Son, that thy Son also may glorify thee.* (John 17:1)

# 11 *The Prayers of Jesus*

The caption, "Handle with Prayer, the World Is Highly Explosive" is an apt one for our times.

Jesus handled every great crisis with prayer, with folded hands, with an indominable spirit, with a submissive attitude. He bathed himself in prayer prior to making any decision. "Watch and pray, that ye enter not into temptation" the Master exhorted his sleepy disciples (Matt. 26:41).

Do you really believe in prayer? The verses of John 17 are truly the Lord's Prayer, rather than what we quote often, which is more accurately "the Model Prayer." I find it hard to read John 17 aloud. It is difficult to identify with the God-man in such dedicated compassion. John, inspired by God, wrote down these tremendous words for us, because evidently no man heard them. It is, without doubt, the most remarkable portion of the most remarkable book in the world.

I wish there was a collection of all the prayers of Jesus, with only the notations as to when and where they were prayed and for what occasion. We tread on sacred ground in Gethsemane when we listen to the Lord's words to his Father. Jesus knew this was the last night of his life. Chapters 13 through 17 of John contain the great prayers of his life, the great loves of his life, the great thoughts of his life, as he tried to bring his beloved friends closer to his heart.

When I read the seventeenth chapter of John, I think about removing my shoes. It is a holy of holies. Jesus completely bared his heart, his soul, his glory. He linked himself in unity with God and with his people. There is a reaching up and a reaching out, and a bringing together of all in one great family of God.

As John Knox lay ill, knowing it was his last illness, he asked his minister friend to read the seventeenth chapter of John every night, for these were the verses that gave him the most comfort and courage.

It has been well written that we should be able to find within these sacred verses our name and our face among these countless ones Jesus was praying for! It is the prayer of prayers, as there is no higher prayer than intercessory prayer. Jesus was interceding for the world with the Most High God, doing his work as our Great High Priest, the only mediator between God and man.

This was one of the very few times when Jesus prayed for himself. Yet he only prayed for himself in relation to others. Already he had tried to prepare his disciples, in the fourteenth chapter, for the death he faced: "I go away, and come again unto you" (John 14:28). He had been speaking words from God to them. In this chapter, we find him speaking to God *for* them.

We are important to God. No person is faceless to him. At some holy moment in this prayer, in that photographic mind and heart of God, there appeared my face and your face, my sins and your sins. "Neither pray I for these alone, but for them also who shall believe on me through their word" Jesus said (John 17:20). He prayed for himself in the first five verses: "Glorify thy son that thy son may glorify thee" (John 17:1). What glory did Jesus desire? The glory "which I had with thee before the world was" (John 17:5). For an example, look back to the mount of transfiguration, when heaven came down in glory upon him, and Moses and Elijah talked with him. John, James, and Peter saw these who descended from heaven. "As they came down from the mountain" Jesus commanded them "that they should tell no man what things they had seen" (Mark 9:9). They were not ready for the glory of God.

Why did Christ desire to be glorified? Not for selfish reasons. We should not grow weary of hearing "God so loved the world that he gave his only begotten Son" (John 3:16). Jesus Christ was God's love-gift to the world, and now the believer, the Christian, these for whom Jesus was praying, he was presenting to the Father as his own. They were Jesus' gift to God: "I pray . . . for them whom thou hast given me; for they are thine" (John 17:9).

What is the glory of God? He spoke of eternal life in the second verse: "that he should give eternal life to as many as thou hast given him." He spoke of his Father's name in the sixth verse: "I have manifested thy name." He spoke of his Father's words in verse 8: "I have given unto them the words which thou gavest me." He spoke of his own joy: "that they might have my joy fulfilled in themselves" (John 17:13). Also, he said, "the glory which thou gavest me I have given them" (John 17:22).

Why did Christ merit this glory? Because he glorified the Father. "I have glorified thee on earth," he said (John 17:4) He glorified him in his life. He glorified him in his miracles. He glorified him in his work and in his words. He came to fulfil the law. Every work that he did was a thing of glory that he presented unto his Father. Not one time did the Father shake his head. "This is my beloved Son, in whom I am well pleased; hear ye him," was the Father's verdict on Jesus' life and work (Matt. 17:5).

On the cross Jesus cried out, "It is finished!" (John 19:30). Yet in this prayer uttered the night before, we find him saying, "I have finished the work which thou gavest me to do" (John 17:4). The glory which the world wanted to see had been shown them: "He that hath seen me hath seen the Father" (John 14:9).

He turned from praying for himself to praying for his disciples and for you and me. He prayed for all those whom the Father had given him. Seven times in this chapter Jesus referred to the fact that God has given us to him. "I pray . . . for them whom thou hast given me" (John 17:9). "I pray not," Jesus said, "that thou shouldest take them out of the world, but that thou shouldest keep them from all evil" (John 17:15). Sometimes we feel that "Stop the earth, I want to get off!" is the way to solve all the problems, but Jesus did not think so.

Then he gave a report of his stewardship: "Those that thou gavest me I have kept, and none of them is lost," he said, "but [and he doesn't even call his name] the son of perdition" (John 17:12). What kind of hurt was in the heart of Jesus as he thought about Judas Iscariot! Even to his Father, who knew all, he qualified why he had lost Judas from the fellowship of disciples.

"All mine are thine, and thine are mine; and I am glorified in them" (John 17:10). He walked with them and talked with them. He shepherded them while he was with them. "Now I am no more in the world," he told his Father, "I come to thee: Holy Father, keep through thine own name those whom thou hast given me" (John 17:11). He placed them back in the Father's hands. Their safety depended upon the Father's grasp.

Jesus had already said to his disciples, "My sheep hear my voice . . . and no man is able to pluck them out of my Father's hand" (John 10:27,29). If I had no reason to believe in eternal life except this prayer of Jesus, I would believe that Jesus' prayer would be answered.

"Sanctify them through thy truth," he prayed; "thy word is truth" (John 17:17). The work of sanctification is a beginning and a continuing state. The prayer of Jesus is actually very simple and relevant, so that nobody could misunderstand.

Dr. James Sullivan said he felt the greatest compliment

ever paid to him in his ministry was when he left his last pastorate, a church which was in the intellectual center of an academic community, and a humble woman came to him. "Dr. Sullivan," she said, "the thing I liked about your messages is that you have never used a word I did not understand. I knew what you were trying to say to me." There was never a moment when Jesus, who is truth, intellectual truth, incarnate truth, did not communicate clearly.

He prayed for himself, for his own, for his church and for its mission. "I pray that they [the church] may be one," he said, "as thou, Father, art in me, and I in thee, that they also may be one in us" (John 17:21). This holy oneness of mind, thought, and desire is what is best for the church.

The great example of oneness of the church of the living God we find when they were all "with one accord in one place" on the day of Pentecost (Acts 2:1). It is unfortunate we have to go back so far into church history to find an example. If only we could be compelled, motivated in an intense desire to share that same oneness—one thought, one purpose, one heart, one prayer, one mission—as they did on the day of Pentecost. Then we would know what Pentecost really was.

Jesus spoke about the glory of God. How can we describe it when we do not know it? Paul, who had seen things unlawful for him to utter, recognized how difficult it would be to describe the glory of heaven. We fall back on that precious promise, "Eye hath not seen, nor ear heard, neither have entered into the heart of man, the things which God has prepared for them that love him" (1 Cor. 2:9). He was talking about the coming great day of culmination, when he would be received back into the hands of the Father. He prayed, "I will that they also, whom thou hast given me, be with me where I am; that they may behold my glory, which thou hast given me" (John 17:24).

Some may cry, moan, pity the church, talk about its failures —if they will. But I still believe in the undimmed glory of the church of God. Jesus shall "present you faultless before the presence of his glory with exceeding joy" (Jude 24).

Yes, Jesus handled every great crisis with prayer. Read again the prayer he prayed in anticipation of his greatest crisis: "These words spoke Jesus, and lifted up his eyes to heaven, and said, Father, the hour is come; glorify thy Son, that thy Son also may glorify thee" (John 17:1).

*Let this mind be in you, which was also in Christ Jesus.*
(Phil. 2:5)

# 12 The Mind of Jesus

The mind is the most delicate mechanism of our physical bodies, and we are "fearfully and wonderfully made" (Ps. 139:14). This mind of ours can be developed, and yet its attitude controls to some extent all the things we do.

The great doctor, Hippocrates, who wrote the oath which physicians still voluntarily subscribe to, said a very significant thing: "Man does not *have* an illness, man *is ill.*" This emphasizes that when a man is ill, he is not compartmentalized. All of him is ill. This is what Paul is saying to us when he asked that we not be satisfied with just thinking like ordinary men, but that we have the mind of Christ—that we be altogether God's.

The expression, "to blow your mind" is often used in our times. But man does not use anything like the limit of his mental powers. The more we study the more we understand. Yet the more we understand, the more we recognize how much more there is to know and how ignorant we are of many important things in life.

The Bible says that Jesus grew in body and mind; he "increased in wisdom and stature, and in favour with God and man" (Luke 2:52). Can we say that he who knew all things actually expanded his mind as he lived upon earth?

The apostle Paul, in his last days, spent most of his time writing from the dungeons of Roman prisons. His letter to the Philippians is often subtitled "the joy of Jesus." Paul used the word "joy" again and again. Finally, at the mountain peak of 2:5 he said, "Let this mind be in you, which was also in Christ Jesus." He holds up before us an example of the Son of God and urges us to be like-minded, to take the same attitude.

The Bible says that a man, "as he thinketh in his heart, so is he" (Prov. 23:7). Our actions mirror our thoughts. We reveal what we are, what we think. Consistently and continually man finds an outlet for his thoughts, whether they are good or evil. If he thinks negatively, he will respond that way. If he thinks positively, usually he will react positively toward life.

After the disastrous earthquake that shook San Francisco in 1907, someone had the vivid imagination to put up a pertinent billboard. In hastily printed letters rising above the broken city were these words, "Don't think earthquake, think business!"

Paul knew this psychological truth. At one time in his ministry he said, "I am the least of the apostles" (1 Cor. 15:9). At another time he said he was "less than the least of all saints" (Eph. 3:8). Then as he began to look inward—after he came face to face with himself, he said that he was the chief of sinners (1 Tim. 1:15). He was growing in the mind of God, because as he measured up to the pattern of God in Christ, he recognized his inadequacy.

Is it possible for a race with so many disunities to come to a unity of mind and purpose? Can the nations of the earth ever agree on anything? Not as long as man goes his own way and thinks his own basically selfish thoughts. The only hope of a united mind is through allegiance to an idea. The ideal of peace can only come through thinking with the mind of Christ. As we have his mind, we shall begin to have his attitudes, or the *disposition* of Christ. What would he do in like situations, in like circumstances, in like position?

We try to imitate what we find in the Bible of him. We can

absorb ourselves in his mind; we can think his thoughts.

Paul said that Christ, "being in the form of God, thought it not robbery to be equal with God" (Phil. 2:6). Think of the person of God! Jesus Christ was one and the same as God. Other passages show there is no separation between Jesus Christ and God the Father and the Holy Spirit. He honored himself, being fashioned as a man and being like God, and yet he honored us in coming to this world, where he "took upon him the form of a servant" (Phil. 2:7). Can you imagine any one of us who has an exalted position doing what Jesus did? The greatest descent in human history is that he who was God took upon himself the form of a servant—even a humble domestic servant, one who actually washed feet.

What more would you ask of God? How could you help but love him? The disciples felt that they were far too important to do anything like that for the others. "After all, I am pretty much the chief spokesman," Peter may have thought. "They ought to be washing my feet." Jesus, who knew their minds, recognized that there wasn't a towel among them. He reached for a towel and took upon himself the task of a servant (see John 13:4–5). There is nothing too little for a great man to do. But there are many things too big for a small man to do.

We have never been anything except men. We have only lived in a physical body. We do not understand how much he gave up to become like us. The angels understood far better than we, for the Bible says he became "a little lower than the angels for the suffering of death" (Heb. 2:9). He who was heavenly became earthly that we who are earthly might possess heavenly things.

Can we ever think like Jesus? We must remember that he who was God became a man and gave us a pattern. Jesus, the carpenter of Nazareth, was truly a pattern maker. First of all, "he humbled himself and became obedient" (Phil. 2:8). The Bible speaks many times about humility. We need to humble ourselves, lest God humble us. It is one thing to be brought to your knees; it is another thing to bend your knees voluntarily. The Bible speaks of his voluntary humiliation.

He "made himself of no reputation" (Phil. 2:7). This is one of the most significant things we will ever find in the Scriptures. There is nothing wrong in our saying we wish to amount to something. We wish to leave this a better world because we passed this way. Jesus made himself of no reputation, but he was constantly enhancing the reputations of others. Is that not the pattern?

Into the court of the Temple one day "there came a certain poor widow, and she threw in two mites"—a meager offering (Mark 12:42). Jesus made her "widow's mite" a household phrase, commemorating an inconspicuous sacrifice. Another woman came and broke her alabaster box. He said, "Wheresoever this gospel shall be preached in the whole world, there shall also this . . . be told for a memorial of her" (Matt. 26:13). He enhanced other people's reputations. You will never go wrong by copying the behavior of Jesus in this matter and in all other ways.

Michelangelo made a reputation as a painter and sculptor. Yet Jesus, who made the colors of the rainbow, made of himself of no reputation. He took the sands of the earth and fashioned the body of man. Michelangelo, with his great ability, never created a man, only imitated the body of a man. He could make the shape of a man as though he could almost speak. But only as God breathed into man the breath of life did he become a living soul. Jesus made no reputation among men as a sculptor. Yet if you took the religious art out of the museums of the earth, the religious pictures out of the books and art galleries, the religious compositions from the world's music, you would have left a great void, because man has to recognize that only God made the originals. Man is able only to copy!

Handel made a great reputation as a musician. Particularly at Christmas all enjoy some of the great music he wrote. But the Lord who formed the vocal chords, and created the wind to give tongue to the reeds on the organ, has no reputation as a musician.

The little shop where Edison invented the incandescent light bulb has been rooted up and brick by brick moved to a museum. Edison brought multiplied light to a dark world. Jesus has no reputation as an electrician, but he claimed boldly, "*I* am the light of the world!" (John 8:12). Then he turned to his disciples (and us) saying, "Ye are the light of the world" (Matt. 5:14). Let this mind be in you! Take the pattern of Jesus!

Dr. Simpson of England discovered chloroform, and now surgical patients do not experience such severe pain. Jesus became the Great Physician. He has come to your heart and mine, to your home and mine, to your life and my life and healed broken hearts without any anaesthesia other than his significant presence. He has rocked us to sleep with tender soothing of spirit. He has refreshed us under the shadow of his wings. The Bible says, "There remaineth therefore a rest to the people of God" (Heb. 4:9).

Napoleon has been remembered as a military genius. Jesus, the "Captain of the Lord's hosts" (Josh. 5:15), taught Joshua how to take Jericho with nothing more than shouting and trumpets, yet Jesus is not known as a military genius. He made himself of no reputation.

He made himself no reputation for being wealthy. He who owned the cattle on a thousand hills had to ask for a penny that he might be able to illustrate what he was teaching (see Mark 12:15). One writer has called Jesus "the greatest tramp of history." That's the kind of reputation he had. No money, no home, no food, no clothing, nothing! He made himself of no reputation. For what purpose? "It became him . . . in bringing many sons unto glory to make the captain of their salvation perfect through sufferings" (Heb. 2:10).

In the sanctuary of your soul, God wants to walk boldly across your mind without encountering closed doors or locked cabinets. There is not a thought God does not know, not one! If we allow him to remold our minds like the mind of Christ, we should reveal him in his love and glory.

What should Jesus' disposition do to us? This humility is not a substitute for laziness. A Christian man is a serving man. Ours should be a trusting mind, leaning on him. Ours should be a steadfast mind, so that we could say with Job, in poverty or wealth, sickness or health, life or death, "Though he slay me, yet will I trust in him" (Job 13:15).

The world is saying they want to know God. The only way they can know God is to experience him in us. Our hands do not bear the scars of Jesus' hands. The only way we can reveal him is to show his mind, his disposition, his likeness. The only thing we can really do is to become like-minded in holy thought and action: "Let this mind be in you."

*And declared to be the Son of God with power, according to the spirit of holiness, by the resurrection from the dead.* (Rom. 1:4)

# 13 *The Sonship of Jesus*

It has been said that in the last ten years more knowledge has accumulated than since the beginning of time. However, Jesus Christ was "the Truth" from the very beginning.

The universal quest of mankind has been to seek truth, to know Jesus, to find God revealed. On that morning of triumphal entry into Jerusalem, Jesus rode quietly, in a modest manner, upon an ass's colt (see John 12:15). The jubilant crowd was enthusiastic. According to Josephus, likely 500,000 people were there. They would have been hanging out the windows, standing on every balcony looking down upon his procession in the narrow street.

"What is the excitement?" they would ask, and "Who is causing all of this?" Now, as then, Jesus comes face to face in a personal encounter with man and asks, "Whom do you say that I, the Son of man, am?" (See Matt. 16:13).

G. K. Chesterton wrote that the only way you can create a good statue is to throw away good marble. If you started to carve the statue of Christ, the likeness of the very Son of God, what would his features be? How could we define his deity? Outside the words of the Bible, we know little about Jesus, historically. We can only know him personally from the days of our conversion. With what words would you describe him?

The Gospels try to picture Jesus, and the apostle Paul said that Jesus "was seen of me also, as of one born out of due time" (1 Cor. 15:8). Each man has put together the picture of Jesus for himself. One may look at his hands and say, "Behold the healing hands of Jesus!" Another would look at his feet and say, "How beautiful . . . are the feet of him that bringeth good tidings!" (Isa. 52:7). Another would look at the wound in his side and say, "He was wounded for our transgressions; he was bruised for our iniquities; the chastisement of our peace was upon him, and with his stripes we are healed" (Isa. 53:5).

A great Presbyterian preacher, Clarence McCartney, was an unusual man of God who was also a great military historian. He drew some parallels between Napoleon and our Savior. From the life of Napoleon he found the very words of Napoleon's confession in his last days. "Jesus is the Son of God. He is the most unique character who ever walked the face of the earth. Other men," said Napoleon, "have built their kingdoms with iron and blood, but he shed no blood other than his own. Other men have destroyed the world, and he has saved the world."

This Christ of contrast, this Prince of Peace, defies any parallels, for there is none other like him. There are good physicians, but he is the Great Physician. There are men of peace, but he is the Prince of Peace. There are some men who are godlike, but he is the Son of God.

The ancient Hebrew race loved to speak of David. Jesus was the son of David. They liked to mention Solomon the wise, but Solomon was the son of a king and Jesus was the Son of God. Solomon was a famous king, but Jesus is the eternal King of kings and Lord of lords. Much wealth and wisdom of this world belonged to Solomon, but Jesus said, "Behold, a greater than Solomon is here" (Luke 11:31). Solomon built the Temple in old Jerusalem. Jesus is building the temple in the new Jerusalem. He said to his desolate band of disciples, "Let not your heart be troubled. . . . I go to prepare a place for you" (John 14:1–2). Is it not a paradox that the Son of God loved best to call himself the Son of man? This was the title he claimed for himself. "Whose son is he?" was the searching personal question.

Jesus looked into the faces of all his disciples and said, "Whom do you say that I, the Son of man, am?" Perhaps he looked particularly into the eyes of Simon. He would probably get a more spontaneous, a more truthful, a more ready answer from him.

Today Jesus looks into our hearts and asks, "Whom do you say that I am?" Each of us must declare whether he is the Son of man only, or the Son of God. The deity of Jesus, the fact that he was virgin-born was no problem to him; he claimed it from his youth. "Wist ye not that I must be about my Father's business?" he asked Mary (Luke 2:49).

There has been discussion in some circles as to whether a man could be a Christian and not believe in the virgin birth. If you cannot believe the virgin birth, then how can you believe he is able to save you? How can you take the word of the Bible concerning the ministry and work and character of Jesus and say you can believe him one time and not believe his claims in another area?

God looked down from heaven at Jesus' baptism and said, "This is my beloved Son, in whom I am well pleased" (Matt. 3:17). I am more interested in who God said he is than any other opinion. Yet while Jesus was in the body he suffered the temptations of the flesh, the difficulties of human life, the aches and pains of daily living. At the same time, he was God incarnate, for the Bible says, "The Word was made flesh, and dwelt amongst us" (John 1:14).

Jesus was preexistant. He said, "Before Abraham was, I am" (John 8:58). His life didn't begin in Bethlehem. Even before God said, "Let there be light!" (Gen. 1:3), Jesus was that light. Even before God said, "Let there be the valleys and the mountains," Jesus was the Rock of Ages. Before there were stars in the sky, Jesus was the Bright and Morning Star.

Before flowers grew on this earth, Jesus was the Lily of the Valley and the Rose of Sharon. The preexistance of Jesus dates to the preexistance of God, for he was the Son of God.

Some said he was simply the son of Mary and Joseph. To some, perhaps, even "father unknown, the son of Mary." Whose son was he? Matthew, knowing the Hebrew mind, was very careful in his genealogy to say that Jesus was "the son of David, the son of Abraham" (Matt. 1:1). Jesus called himself "the Son of man" (Luke 19:10) Whose son is he? With Simon Peter, I believe "Thou art the Christ, the Son of the living God" (Matt. 16:16).

His unusual birth indicated he was the Son of God. The manner in which he was able to die indicated that he was the Son of God. His resurrection from the tomb indicated that he was the Son of God. At his baptism, the descent of the Holy Spirit from heaven indicated that he was the Son of God. His ascension, when he was received back into the portals of heaven, indicated that he was the Son of God.

There is ample evidence of his supernatural power. There is ample evidence in the Bible. Surely there is ample evidence in your own relationship to Christ, to recognize that he has supernatural power. Have you not heard? Have you not prayed? Have you not experienced it?

His contemporaries were conscious of his power during his ministry. They recognized that he had unusual power. The problem was that they said it was not the power of God, it could be the power of Satan (see Luke 11:15). They looked at him and said, "Who is he?"

In those days following his triumphant entry into Jerusalem, they looked at him as he stood before Pilate who, "when he had scourged Jesus, delivered him to be crucified" (Matt. 27:26). At his resurrection, there was display of his supernatural power. In the next forty days following, "then were his disciples glad, when they saw the Lord" (John 20:20). He was able to go through closed doors, to appear and disappear. He was the supernatural Son of Mary, for this was the only time in the history of the world where a person was born without an earthly father. He was the supernatural Son of Mary and he was the supernatural Son of God. God verified his claims repeatedly. "I am Alpha and Omega, the beginning and the ending," he said in the last book in the Bible "who is, and who was, and who is to come, the Almighty" (Rev. 1:8).

He was supernatural, for he said, "Behold, I am alive for evermore, Amen; and have the keys of hell and death" (Rev. 1:18). He claimed supernatural power when he said, "the Son of man hath power on earth to forgive sins" (Matt. 9:6). When he said this, the Jews asked, "Why doth this man thus speak blasphemies? Who can forgive sins but God only?" (Mark 2:7). They had eyes to see and could not see, ears to hear and could not hear.

The supernatural Son of God, the supernatural Savior—what does he mean historically? He came to reveal God. His identification as the only begotten Son of God has a unique meaning. Not only was he the only Son, but the only Son that God ever has had, ever will have, that was ever in the power and capacity of God to have—the supernatural Son of God, having the "glory as of the only-begotten of the Father, full of grace and truth" (John 1:14).

What is the right concept of Jesus? Men today make out of him a radical leader. Men today make out of him a changer of the *status quo,* and some make him slightly more than a social worker. But the greatest thing he came to do was to save mankind and to reveal God's boundless love.

In the Old Testament, a major concept of God was one of anger, wrath, and judgment. Jesus came and walked among men in love, not in opposition to the character of God, but in order to clarify it in the minds and hearts of men. They could not fully understand the character of God until it was revealed in the face of Christ. He said to his disciples, "Have I been so long time with you, and yet hast thou not known . . . ? He that hath seen me hath seen the Father. . . . I and my Father are one!" (John 14:9; 10:30). In other words, "I am disappointed that you cannot understand the character of God, for I have come to reveal him."

What claims did Jesus make concerning his ministry, his motives, his mastery of life? For what reason did he come? The angel said to Mary, "Thou shalt conceive, . . . and bring forth a son, and shalt call him Jesus," (Luke 1:31). To Joseph the name was further explained, "for he shall save his people from their sins" (Matt. 1:21). The songwriter took as his title, "Jesus Is the Sweetest Name I Know!" Jesus, the winsome one to every heart, the acclamation of every soul, the decision of every life. Jesus came, not just that you might have more clothes, not just that you might have a whole body, not just that you might be better liked, not just that you might have a more abundant life. "The Son of man is come to seek and to save that which was lost" (Luke 19:10). We are worth all the world to him.

Salvation is not to be found in works, but only in Jesus. "Neither is there salvation in any other: for there is no other name under heaven given among men, whereby we must be saved" (Acts 4:12).

Only one word opens the doors of heaven, and that is the name of Jesus. You can knock on the door with wealth in your hand, and it will remain closed. You can knock on the door with works in your hand, and the voice from heaven will never answer. Only if you claim Jesus will the door be opened.

The Son of God said, "Whosoever, therefore, shall confess me before men, him will I confess also before my Father, who is in heaven" (Matt. 10:32). Whose Son is he—to you?

*And when the Pharisees saw it, they said unto his disciples, Why eateth your Master with publicans and sinners?*
(Matt. 9:11)

# 14 The Friendship of Jesus

On one occasion Jesus said to his disciples, "Henceforth, I call you not servants; . . . but I have called you friends" (John 15:15). This is a very wonderful relationship. Wouldn't you have liked to be there and heard it from his own lips? The best-attested fact in the New Testament is that Jesus is my friend and yours. If we had no other reason to believe it, Calvary would prove it.

The story in Matthew 9 showed Jesus' position toward the social and religious prejudices of his day. It pointed out, as few other incidents of his ministry, his reason for coming into the world. He was fellowshiping with a man identified by the Jews as a traitor, a sinner. He spent more time with such people than with those who made a habit of religious observances. What kind of friend was Jesus?

A person in deep sorrow said, "God is no friend of mine, to let this happen to me!" Of course, we say things in such moments of shock, sometimes, that we do not really mean. We ought to remember this—and friends ought to be careful to understand it.

Jesus fulfilled the Old Testament proverb that "there is a friend that sticketh closer than a brother" (Prov. 18:24). This meant a great deal in biblical days, when kinship—family and clan relationships, were more important than in our day. Jesus fulfilled also the psalm, "When my father and my mother forsake me [or your brothers or sisters or children], then the Lord will take me up" (Ps. 27:10). Have we realized that the greatest man who ever walked, the most perfect man who ever lived, is the best friend that sinners ever had? Aside from the logical conclusion of Calvary, there are several things we can look at in his life and ministry.

First of all, he was called a friend of tax-collectors and sinners (see Matt. 11:19). We are grateful that we can say we are saved by his grace. I know Jesus is our friend because he identified himself with us and died for our sin. Go through all the sayings of Jesus, and you will find that he was never hard on sinners, but always hard on their sin. "Neither do I condemn thee: go, and sin no more," he said to the woman taken in adultery (John 8:11). He told his disciples, "The thief cometh not but to steal, and to kill, and to destroy: I am come that they might have life, and that they might have it more abundantly!" (John 10:10). Jesus' words, even taken out of context, never intimate that he was the foe of a man, but he was always the foe of sin. There is a vast difference!

Sometimes we get that principle confused. Jesus proved himself, his words show this! Never did he argue against the person of any man, but in every way he showed each their need of him. His life showed that he is our friend.

The word "compassion" is a strong New Testament word that we use often. It means "to suffer with": he suffers with me—that is the complete meaning of it. Now there is a great difference between feeling sorry for someone and having identifying sympathy with them.

You have heard it fliply said, "I can feel for you, but I can't reach you!" Jesus not only felt for us; he can reach us! This was the problem of the man robbed and beaten on the Jericho road. He could see the men who passed him by, and they could see him, but his plight just didn't reach them. A Samaritan got down, and came where he was, and helped him (see Luke 10:33).

Jesus did not ever apologize for associating with the poor,

the outcast, the sinful. This was not the only time they accused him. They said Jesus was "a gluttonous man" because he liked to eat and attended banquets. They even said he was "a winebibber" (Luke 7:34). Because he associated with sinners, they made him guilty by association. "If he were as good as we are," they implied, "He would pay attention to us, he wouldn't go down there where they are!" Are we friends to people when they need friends, or are we friends to people when we want friends? Friendship is a two-way street, but some folks want to travel it in only one direction. Jesus' compassion demonstrated where his heart was.

He didn't say to Matthew, for instance, "Matthew, I want to be your friend, but you must realize my position. I cannot afford to be identified with you because you are a tax collector, and most people despise you. If I am your friend, they will criticize me!" Jesus always chose the side of humanity. Matthew and Zacchaeus were probably some of the loneliest men of their day. Jesus was severely criticized for going to their houses, but he accepted the criticism and went right on being the friend of sinners.

He showed compassion for the whole city, and wept over it, not just because of some few there, but because all of them were his concern. All of them were his friends, and he mourned over even the Pharisees, saying, "all ye are brethren" (Matt. 23:8).

Mr. Colgate, when he died a few years ago, was the wealthy head of a large corporation. He came to New York City when he was a very young man, having lived in a smaller town upstate. He traveled on a ship through the lakes and rivers, and they had to stop at each lock. A man hauling freight on the ship let young Colgate help pay his passage by assisting him with the extra work entailed in going through the locks.

"What are you going to do when you get to New York?" the man asked.

"I don't know," young Colgate said.

"Well, what have you done?" the man inquired.

"The only thing I know how to do is to make soap," Colgate replied.

"Then, son," the man advised as they parted in New York, "make the best soap that you can sell for a profit, and give God a tenth of every penny you make!"

As a boy, Mr. Colgate observed this honorable man over a period of several days, and he took his advice. During his lifetime, Mr. Colgate gave much money to charitable and missionary causes because of the impression he received from this layman: "make the best soap you can and give God a tenth." Mr. Colgate built his church a beautiful Gothic structure, a memorial to a member of his family.

One morning, a woman came into the services and made a public profession of faith in Christ. She was well known and had a poor reputation in the community. They stammered and hesitated over a motion to admit her to membership. Mr. Colgate stood up.

"Gentlemen," he said, "I am ashamed. We have been praying for God to save somebody, and now that God has, we are not joyful about it. We're all just 'respectable sinners,' ourselves. I want to apologize to this woman because we haven't had the spirit of Jesus and the friendship of Jesus. If she will forgive us, I, for one, will act as a friend of Jesus toward her as long as she wishes to attend."

Jesus never took his respect away from anybody. He never took his love away from anybody. Men spurned him, but he never spurned mankind. To have such a friend is a wonderful thing.

Usually, we are kidding ourselves if we think we have a lot of friends, although we may know a lot of people. Count as friends only those who are with you when you are down as well as when you are up, when you are wrong as well as when you are right. "I don't condemn you," Jesus says to us. "I encourage you in a better way of life." Isn't it incredible? The most perfect man who ever lived is willing to offer those who are so imperfect his friendship! Yet we, forgetting our own shortcomings, often judge with severity other imperfect people.

A student pastor went to visit a young farmer who had recently returned from military service. He was plowing, and the preacher went to the last furrow and waited for him. After they talked a while, the young preacher said, "Do you realize the Lord could save you right now in the cool of this freshly plowed row?" Then he suggested, "Let's kneel here," and knelt in the raw earth.

The young farmer knelt, also, and bowed his head. Soon, in prayer, he turned his life over to Jesus. Afterward, he expressed his thanks over and over.

"If you wanted to be a Christian so badly, and if you are so glad to be a Christian now, why weren't you a Christian before?" the preacher asked curiously.

"Plenty of preachers have come over here and told me what a rough life I lived in the army." The young farmer looked up sharply. "I don't know whether you knew that or not, but you didn't say a word about it! All you did was tell me that Jesus loves me."

Unfortunately, his mother and father had been condemning him, also. They had a list of "thou shalt nots," which gave their son no reassurance that God loved him in spite of his sin.

"I had begun to wonder if Jesus really did love me, and that's what I wanted to know."

God doesn't turn his back on us! If a back is turned, we can be sure it is ours. The people to whom we need to witness are no different from what we were before God saved us.

Jesus came into the world, bearing all God's love, to pour it out on Calvary for sinful men—together with his life's blood. Oh, his friendship to us is wonderful!

*Then saith he to Thomas, Reach hither thy finger, and behold my hands; and reach hither thy hand, and thrust it into my side: and be not faithless, but believing.*
(John 20:27)

# 15 *The Touch of Jesus*

A woman with a serious illness reached out and touched the Master. She thought no one saw her; no one knew she had reached out and touched his garment. Quickly, there came a response from Jesus, "Who touched me?" (Luke 8:45).

The touch of our Lord—how powerful, how helpful, how wonderful!

When we think of touch, we usually think concerning nearness. How far away is God? Is he near or far? In Job's desperate plight, he groped in darkness for comprehension: "Oh, that I knew where I might find him!" (Job 23:3). He was not sure of the direction of God, the nearness of God, or even the availability of God. But he was in earnest, and God revealed himself.

We recognize there is a great separation between God and man, a separation caused by sin. Because sin came into the world, Adam and Eve hid from God. As Isaiah said, "Your iniquities have separated between you and your God" (Isa. 59:2).

However, at present there is a clear invitation from God, a great hope, the insistence of Jesus, and the promise, "Draw nigh to God, and he will draw nigh to you" (Jas. 4:8).

The woman at the well in Samaria admitted to Jesus that she knew she ought to worship God, but "Our fathers worshiped in this mountain; and ye say that in Jerusalem is the place where men ought to worship" (John 4:20). Jesus drove home the great definition of the Godhead when he said, "God is a Spirit; and they that worship him must worship him in spirit and in truth" (John 4:24). If God is Spirit, then how shall we touch him?

It is not so much our touching God, but rather it is our drawing near to God so that he may touch us. Of course, we recognize the touch of God is another one of those marvelous, expressive symbols that indicate his loving care.

Nothing carries any more intimacy, or any more promise, than a touch. Nothing is quieter, and nothing is more exciting than the touch of the Lord. Paradoxically, the touch of God may be a tender touch—as tender as the touch of a child with its smooth face and chubby hands—or the strong hand of God's judgment upon mankind. The psalmist tells us the hand of God can be a heavy hand: "day and night thy hand was heavy upon me" (Ps. 32:4). When the hand of God moves against us and over on us, we are conscious of a God to be feared.

Amos said, describing God's anger against his sinful nation, "the Lord God of hosts . . . toucheth the land, and it shall melt" (Amos 9:5).

"Have pity upon me, O ye my friends," Job cried out, "for the hand of the Lord hath touched me!" (Job 19:21).

Have you ever been a witness? "Describe the man," someone may say to you. What would you say? Well, you'd probably mention, if you could recall, his height, coloring, features, characteristics. But there is a passage that we find in 1 Samuel 10:26 where we read that there went with Saul "a band of men, whose hearts God had touched." Describe these men—can you?

The Scripture mentions nothing of their intellect or wisdom, nothing of their wealth or strength. What does God describe? It seems that what God considered the important thing about these men was that they were men whose hearts

God had touched.

When God looks down on us, I am not sure he notices whether your suit is black or brown, but I do know he looks into your heart. The prophet said, "The heart is deceitful above all things, and desperately wicked, who can know it?" (Jer. 17:9). What is the only cure? The touch of God on our hearts.

The touch of God is a cleansing touch. God had to make a great transformation to bring sinners into the presence of his holiness. It took a miracle, a miracle of love and grace. Only God could touch these lives of ours and make them acceptable in his sight.

We see many advertisements of detergents, but bear in mind that the only thing that makes a difference in our lives is the cleansing power of the blood of Christ. The songwriter has raised the question and answered it:

> What can wash away my sin?
> Nothing but the blood of Jesus.
> What can make me whole again?
> Nothing but the blood of Jesus.

Sometimes we see the stark ugliness of nature in winter. Then comes filtering down from the sky the blanketing snow. Soon the ugliness is hidden by the beautifying touch of God. The Bible raises the question, "Hast thou entered into the treasures of the snow?" (Job 38:22). That's what we're talking about when we talk about salvation! "Though your sins be as scarlet, they shall be as white as snow; though they be red like crimson, they shall be as wool" (Isa. 1:18). The cleansing energy of God is the sacrificial blood of Jesus Christ on Calvary. This makes the difference, and man's soul is white as snow before God. How wonderful to realize that God is able to cleanse us and make us whole! It is almost more than man can comprehend.

A man who was suffering from leprosy came to Jesus and pled, "Lord, if thou wilt, thou canst make me clean."

"I will, be thou clean!" Jesus said. Out of the cleansing ability of God, this man became whole.

Two blind men cried out to Jesus, "Thou son of David, have mercy on us!" (Matt. 9:27). According to their faith, they were cured. The touch of Jesus is a healing, illuminating touch. It is the only thing that can root out old attitudes, old sins, old lives and make us new again.

The touch of Jesus is not only convicting, but comforting. When the disciples were with Jesus on Galilee in a boat, they were full of anxiety because of a severe storm. They felt they were about to sink, drown, die. They turned to the Master in the selfsame way we often do, feeling that God knows nothing about the circumstances. In impatient lack of faith they said, "Master, carest thou not that we perish?" (Mark 4:38). When Jesus spoke, the wind and the waves obeyed his will, and immediately there was a great calm. There are times when God has touched us and brought calmness, stilling our storm, calming our turmoil, making a difference in all of the difficult circumstances in our lives. Jesus still can command, "Peace, be still!" in our lives.

Jesus used his hands to comfort illness. Peter's wife's mother lay very sick with a fever. Jesus touched her, and she was comforted, strengthened, and ready for service (Mark 1:30–31). Any time we are touched by the Lord, in any circumstance, there is always comfort.

Jesus said to a man who lay by the pool of Bethesda, "Wilt thou be made whole?" (John 5:6).

"How can I?" the man complained. "I have no man . . . to put me into the pool." Jesus touched him with a word of mercy and healing and lifted him up.

A man who was not a Jew came to Jesus and said, "Lord, my servant lieth at home sick." Jesus said he would go, but the centurion replied, "But speak the word only, and my servant shall be healed."

Jesus marveled aloud. "I have not found so great faith, no, not in Israel!" (Matt. 8:6–10).

There are those who toss on beds of illness. We recognize that all healing is divine, the touch of God, the work of mercy. God uses the talent of dedicated people to heal these bodies of ours. We should call on God as we would call on man, to do that which man cannot do. Man can minister to the body in a limited sort of way for some threescore and ten years—but that is all.

Then there is even greater need, for which we must have a greater physician. He must be one who can touch the heart. He must be one who can minister to the soul. Men cannot do this. Only the Great Physician can do something about hurt hearts. Only he can make the difference between life and death. Only the Great Physician can say, "My peace I give unto you! . . . Let not your heart be troubled" (John 14:27).

The greatest picture of worship in the Bible is found in the sixth chapter of Isaiah. This prince of Israel said, as he stood before the altar confessing to God, "I am a man of unclean lips, and I dwell in the midst of a people of unclean lips." The seraphim took a live coal from the altar and "laid it upon my mouth, and said, Lo, . . . thine iniquity is taken away and thy sin is purged." He was pure before God. Then he looked up into heaven and saw God in the midst of all his glory. The Lord said, "Whom shall I send, and who will go for us?"

"Here am I; send me!" Isaiah responded (Isa. 6:5–8).

When there is a fresh touch from God, there comes a new surge of intent. We are challenged by the closeness of our relationship with God. Somehow we forget those things we were going to ask the Lord to do for us. We simply say, "O God, what can I do for you?" That's a test of whether we are close to God or far away: "Here am I, send me!"

How long has it been since the Lord touched you? There were three servants to whom their master entrusted sums of money. The man who had received only one talent said, when he was asked for an accounting, "I was afraid, and went and hid thy talent in the earth" (Matt. 25:25). There are many of us who do not move out in the way God directs because we somehow have lost contact, we have lost touch. We are afraid—not afraid of the dark, not fearful of others, but fearful of ourselves—of our own inadequacy, of our own mistakes, of our own failures. He said what many of us feel, very often, "I was afraid."

Would you let God touch you so that you would not be fearful to attempt what God wants you to do? Surely, if God wishes you to do it, he can enable you, as he promised Moses, "Now therefore go, and I will be with thy mouth" (Ex. 4:12). "Our sufficiency is of God," Paul said (2 Cor. 3:5). God gives ability to the individual. If God has some task for you, God has also the touch to enable you to do it! Be not afraid—except of our sins, as we stand in the presence of God.

Thomas, the disciple who was absent the first time Jesus appeared to them in his resurrected body, had said, "Except I shall see in his hands the print of the nails, . . . I will not believe!" (John 20:25).

"All right, Thomas, touch me!" Jesus challenged him. "If that's your need, take hold of me and see if I am not real!" Thomas fell at his feet and worshiped him, saying, "My Lord and my God!"

Jesus said to the woman in the crowd, "Who touched me?" Perhaps we all think that we may be unnoticed down here somewhere in the acres of God's world, that God loses us in the crowd, that he cannot hear our prayers and be conscious of our individual needs.

But God is waiting for your outstretched hand that he might reach down with his touch of healing, of strength, of power. It is that blessing from him, that renewal, that dedication, that empowering, that we need for all the demands of our lives.

*Jesus said unto them, If God were your Father, ye would love me: for I proceeded forth and came from God; neither came I of myself, but he sent me.*

(John 8:42)

# 16 The Claims of Jesus

There came a time when Jesus demanded, "Who do men say that I am?"

His disciples replied, "Some say that thou art John the Baptist; some, Elijah, and others, Jeremiah, or one of the prophets."

"But who say ye that I am?" Jesus persisted.

Simon Peter answered, "Thou art the Christ, the Son of the living God" (see Matt. 16:13–16).

What claims did Jesus Christ make for himself? It has been said he never claimed to be God, but they must not have read their Bibles. He made claims about his life, his ministry, and his mission that are some of the most startling made by anyone that ever walked the earth.

"Heaven and earth shall pass away," he said, "but my words shall not pass away" (Mark 13:31). On the tempestuous Sea of Galilee, "even the winds and the sea obey him," his disciples testified (Matt. 8:27).

C. S. Lewis said that Jesus gives you no neutral ground, and I agree.

"Well, I can't accept Jesus as the Son of God," some say, "but I'll go along with the fact that he was a good, moral teacher." How could you accept a man as a moral teacher you couldn't trust? He claimed to have the power of God: "All power is given to me in heaven and in earth" (Matt.

28:18). If he was not God, he was either dishonest and unscrupulous, or a madman! You have to believe him as God, or you have to write him off completely.

One critic wrote concerning Jesus that "He was the supreme egoist of all mankind."

"I, if I be lifted up from the earth, will draw all men unto me" (John 12:32)—the entire world! That was his claim, that was his offer, that was his affirmation.

He said to the Jews, "The Son of man is Lord also of the sabbath" (Luke 6:5)—this infuriated them. He said, "Destroy this temple, and in three days I will raise it up" (John 2:19)—this exasperated them. He demonstrated his power over demons, and this they could not understand.

The Bible says he was born of a virgin: "That which is conceived in her is of the Holy Spirit" (Matt. 1:20). He came from heaven for one purpose, to redeem sinful mankind. He was the suffering one of Isaiah 53. He was the glorified one of Revelation 1:8, "I am Alpha and Omega, the beginning and the end." He's the one of whom we sing that "He's the lily of the valley, the bright and morning star."

Usually, he spoke of himself as the Son of man. He also said that he was the Son of God made flesh. It was the greatest human event in history when "The Word was made flesh, and dwelt among us" (John 1:14). It is beyond the comprehension of man to realize that God could take upon himself the form of Adam.

Jesus claimed he was born of a virgin, that his Father was God. That his mother, Mary, had known no man, an angel attested to Joseph. How old is Jesus? The world celebrates his birthday when he was born in Bethlehem, but he said, "Before Abraham was, I am." (John 8:58). He was the "Lamb slain from the foundation of the world" (Rev. 13:8).

Jesus was the God-man. Do not take him out of his humanity as he approached the cross. He hungered, he thirsted, he was tested; he knew all the problems of mankind.

Once, as I was describing the loneliness of Jesus in an

informal group, a man spoke up and said, "Do you mean to say that he was a man as lonely as I am, as hungry as I have been, as tempted as I have been?"

"Yes," I replied, "that's what we mean." That's exactly what Jesus went through, for the Bible says that he was "made of a woman" (Gal. 4:4) and "he was in all points tempted like as we are" (Heb. 4:15).

"The foxes have holes, and the birds of the air have nests," he said, "but the Son of man hath not where to lay his head" (Matt. 8:20). I don't think his head had as hard a time as his heart did. He couldn't feel at home in this world. He was homeless in this life. It was true at his birth, it was also true the day of his burial. He was born in a borrowed stable and laid to rest in a borrowed tomb.

Strangely, Plato said, about a hundred years before Jesus was born, that "if ever a perfect man should be born in this world, the world would kill him, because they wouldn't want to see the contrast!"

Jesus challenged his critics, "Which one of you convicteth me of sin?" But they tried to stone him, just the same. Pilate said, "I find no fault in this man" (Luke 23:4). Yet the crowd demanded that he be crucified. He was not *a* Son of man, he was *the* Son of man.

I hesitate to use the term, "the divinity of Jesus." I think it is better now to refer to "the deity of Jesus." The universal ists have perverted the doctrines of the Bible so that not all of us mean the same thing by "divinity." Some talk about the divinity of man, but unless God is in you, there's not much divinity there. The Bible says, "There is none righteous, no, not one!" (Rom. 3:10).

Jesus claimed to be the Son of God, but far more important is that God claimed him as his Son. Out by the river Jordan, when he was baptized, the Holy Spirit descended from heaven upon him in the form of a dove, and from the balconies of heaven God leaned over and said, "Thou art my beloved Son, in whom I am well pleased" (Mark 1:11). On the mount of transfiguration, God told Jesus' disciples, "This is my beloved Son; hear ye him!" (Mark 9:7).

When Mary and Joseph brought the infant Jesus into the Temple on the fortieth day after his birth in Bethlehem, Simeon looked at the pink little child and saw beyond, to the thirty-third year of his life and said, "Lord, . . . mine eyes have seen thy salvation" (Luke 2:30).

Jesus is the precious one of God's promises. In the day of disaster, God said to the serpent, "I will put enmity between thee and the woman, and between thy seed and her seed; it shall bruise thy head, and thou shalt bruise his heel" (Gen. 3:15). He was the prophesied one: in the dark days of the Old Testament, Isaiah said, "Behold, a virgin shall conceive, and bear a son, and shall call his name Immanuel [God with us]!" (Isa. 7:14).

Consider the claim, "I am the door!" (John 10:7), and "I am the way, the truth, and the life; no man cometh unto the Father, but by me" (John 14:6).

"A greater than Solomon is here," he asserted (Luke 11:31). Greater than Solomon—the wisest man that ever walked the face of the earth? Why not? For he was doing the will of the Father; he was doing the work of the Father, he was showing forth the wisdom of the Father.

The woman at the well of Sychar asked in wonderment, "Art thou greater than our father, Jacob?" (John 4:12). Jesus offered her living water, and she believed. The Pharisees sneered, "Art thou greater than our father, Abraham?" The Son of God replied, "Before Abraham was, I am!" (John 8: 53,58).

Pilate asked him in court, "Art thou the King of the Jews?" Jesus did not deny it, but said, "My kingdom is not of this world" (John 18:33,36).

His coming was the greatest redeeming event of the world. "Thou shalt call his name Jesus," Joseph was told, "for he shall save his people from their sin" (Matt. 1:21). He said of himself that "the Son of man is come to seek and to save that which was lost" (Luke 19:10).

Paul said that Jesus, "who knew no sin," was made "to be sin for us, that we might be made the righteousness of God in him" (2 Cor. 5:21). Crucified like other men, he died and was buried, but he rose from the grave like the Son of God he said he was. The grave is the great leveller; it challenges all claims of mankind.

Other men have claimed they would live after death, but Jesus actually lived again. Luke said that he "showed himself alive" (Acts 1:3). He came to save, he lived to save, he died to save; he was resurrected and is now in heaven interceding for us, our great High Priest (Heb. 4:14). What did a priest do in the Old Testament? He went among the people on behalf of God, as God's servant. Then he went into the holy of holies once a year and showed himself to God on behalf of the people. It was a sacred hour when he took the blood from the altar to sprinkle on the mercy-seat. The people could hear him as he moved about in his priestly garments because of the bells tinkling on the hem of his robe.

The offering he made was on behalf of the people, praying with them that it might be acceptable to God. There was a rope on one ankle, always, because if he died back there, they couldn't go after him—that was where God dwelt! The rope was so that he could be pulled out, but as long as the bells could be heard, they knew he was still alive and God was accepting their offering.

Jesus Christ, the Bible tells us, went into the holy of holies in heaven once for all (Heb. 9:24). In the greatest drama of human history, he became the sacrifice, shown to the people as the provision of God, his servant for their sake as he went to the cross. Then he presented himself to God in heaven after his resurrection, the acceptable sacrifice to whom all other sacrifices pointed.

Jesus became our sin-offering. The veil of the temple was rent and the holy of holies exposed, because the veil was needed no longer. Through Christ, the way of access to God was open for everyone, and he was "declared to be the Son of God with power, . . . by the resurrection from the dead" (Rom. 1:4).

The Son of God made one last claim which has not yet been fulfilled: "I will come again" (John 14:3). His second coming will be the greatest climactic event of the world.

Forty days after his resurrection, Jesus Christ, looking like the same man with whom they had lived for three years, took his followers out to the Mount of Olives. He ascended into the heavens before their awestruck eyes. Then "two men stood by them in white apparel" who said, "This same Jesus, who is taken up from you into heaven, shall so come in like manner as ye have seen him go into heaven" (Acts 1:10–11).

Indescribable is the love, the mercy, the nature, the character, and the wisdom of God. His divine plan has always been, "Yet have I set my king upon my holy hill of Zion" (Ps. 2:6). To Jesus Christ all knees will bow, "For he must reign, till he hath put all enemies under his feet" (1 Cor. 15:25).

"All things were created by him and for him" the apostle Paul said. "And he is before all things, and by him all things consist" (Col. 1:16–17). Now and for all eternity, the God-man is seated in the heavenly throne at God's right hand, and in him God has chosen to sum up and head up all creation.

The last promise in the Bible is that of the risen Christ who said, "Surely, I come quickly!" As his other words have been, this claim, also, will be fulfilled in the personal Jesus, who is *for* us and *with* us and will receive us into his glory. Why? "That where I am," he said to those who followed him, "there ye may be also!" That is the personal promise of the personal Jesus!

*And thou shalt have joy and gladness; and many shall rejoice at his birth.* (Luke 1:14)

# 17 The Love of Jesus

In a certain community in the Southeastern United States the "meanest" woman in town met Jesus Christ. "Mean Mrs. McArthur" the children used to call her, though McArthur was not her real name (my brother in the pastorate, who shared her story with me, never told me her real name). She lived in a small house at the edge of town, and she lived alone. Nobody liked her, and apparently she returned the feeling; she was never known to have any friends. How she got the reputation of being "mean" was something of a puzzle to my brother pastor. When he pressed members of the community for specific instances of Mrs. McArthur's meanness, no one could recall any. But there Mrs. McArthur was: sour, embittered, lonely and unloved. Then she met Jesus Christ, met him on a bright, cold, crisp February Sunday morning at an ordinary eleven o'clock worship service. Not in some special revival meeting. Not with some visiting evangelist preaching. But in an ordinary Sunday morning worship service with the pastor bringing the message.

Now my brother pastor is no great shakes as a preacher. If you want to be charitable, you can say that he makes an earnest effort to deliver the gospel message. He is the kind of preacher who "worries" a text in much the same way that a hungry West Texas dog will "worry" a soupbone. It is a good thing that our Lord's return is not conditional upon my brother pastor's homiletical ability; I fear we would have to wait long for the millennium. But my brother pastor loves Jesus. When he talks about the Lord, he glows. It is almost as though someone had turned on a lightbulb inside his face. You forget his difficulties in getting the meaning of the holy Scriptures into the prosaic words of the English language. You see only his love for Jesus. (Come to think of it, maybe he *is* a pretty good preacher at that. After all, if we preachers get across our love for Jesus, we will make a very good impact on our world.) But it is only kind to say that an ordinary Sunday morning worship service in his church is likely to be just that—ordinary.

Yet Mrs. McArthur met Jesus at just such an ordinary worship service on Sunday morning.

There is this about meeting Jesus, friend: when you meet the Savior, *really* meet the Savior, something is going to happen, and something is going to change. It does not matter how many times you have heard about Jesus before. It does not matter how many times you have been in church. It does not matter how old you are, or how young you are, or even where and who you are. When you meet Jesus, something is going to happen, and something is going to change.

It happened to Mrs. McArthur, and she was the one who changed. Changed the way people change when they meet Jesus. Changed the way people change when they live for Jesus. Changed the way people change when they love Jesus and know that Jesus loves them.

You see, this personal Jesus of mine—this personal Jesus who can be yours if you will let him be so—this personal Jesus is a loving Jesus. There's an old saying that love makes the world go 'round; it could be better amended to say: love makes the heart beat with God's.

Before long, Mrs. McArthur found out what it was like to have her heart beat with God's heart, and she was no longer the "meanest" woman in town. (I put "mean" in quotes because I have an idea that Mrs. McArthur never really was "mean" at all; I think that she was just a lonely and unloved person, lonely and lost as multiplied thousands are today—as perhaps even you who read this are at this very moment.) No, Mrs. McArthur had found the love of Jesus, that love that is generous, gentle, joyous.

The love of Jesus is generous. It is freely offered, freely given to him who will take. My brethren in the pastorate may raise questions about the text I have chosen for this chapter that deals with "The Love of Jesus," but I think a moment's searching of their memories, a moment's recalling of lives changed on the church field will bring understanding. Let us hear the Scripture: "And thou shalt have joy and gladness; and many shall rejoice at his birth (luke 1:14)." The Scripture, of course, refers *not* to the birth of our Lord, Jesus, but to the birth of the great Forerunner, John the Baptist. It is within this context: The aged priest, Zacharias, has gone into the temple to burn incense according to the custom of his priest's office. An angel of the Lord appears to him from the right side of the altar and tells him that the priest's equally aged wife, Elizabeth, will conceive and bear a son whom they are to name John. This son, sent of God, is to go in the spirit and power of Elijah. Malachi 4:5–6 had promised that God would send Elijah before the great "day of the Lord"; John is to go in this spirit and power, and thereby is the role anticipated in Malachi to be fulfilled. John. Why John? Why would the angel tell Zacharias that he was to name the expected son John? The name means "God is gracious."

How generous God is with his grace! Many a heart—like that of Mrs. McArthur—needs to be prepared for Jesus to come in. Many a heart is like one of these Texas broncs we have out here in the Southwest; friend, you try to be the first man to saddle and ride one of these cayuses and you will appreciate the necessity for a good saddlehorse being properly "prepared." The job of John the Baptist was to prepare the hearts of Israel for the One who would come. As far as we know from the record, he did just that. But nothing in that record connects him with love. Nothing is said about the love of John the Baptist. But a great deal is said about the love of Jesus. "God is love," saith the Scriptures. Over and over that love is demonstrated in the life and words of Jesus. It is a generous love.

I have a preacher friend who held a revival in Florida. He did a good work for the Lord. The church where he preached was small and rural.

The last day of the revival services, half a dozen men, at various times during the day, approached my friend and asked him to drop by the house before he left to drive back to North Carolina. This he did. Each time he was given a bushel or two of Florida fruit. My friend tells me these persons were very generous—so generous in fact that, as he drove back North, the back end of his car loaded with Florida fruit, the low beams of his headlights were tilted so much they were pointing at the North Star all the way home.

Generous.

Peter and John, apostles who knew the love of Jesus, were coming out of the Temple when they met a lame man begging. Silver and gold had they none, but that which they did have, they gave generously: "In the name of Jesus of Nazareth, rise up and walk!"

Generous.

Bill Wallace could have lived out his life in the beautiful state of Tennessee, a respected Christian doctor and a useful Christian citizen. But he chose instead to pour out that life for Jesus in a far-off province of China, finally giving up life itself—the ultimate generosity, the ultimate love—in a Communist prison cell. All because he knew the generous love of a personal Jesus.

Generous.

The love of Jesus is a generous love.

I believe it was Dr. R. G. Lee who first saw a gospel application in the following footnote from history.[1] In 1875 the Erie Railroad was extending track at a place called Ararat Summit when a quarter of a mile of railroad track and roadbed disappeared completely. The area turned into a great quagmire in place of solid ground. The Erie people were determined to lay a railroad track through the area and decided to spare no expense in its construction. It is said that they poured ten thousand carloads of gravel and 500 large hemlock trees into the morass—all to no avail. Finally they dug down to solid rock, 160 feet below the surface. On this solid rock they constructed four tiers of pilings, each forty feet long. The construction required 1,500 trees and the equivalent of a hill of gravel. The railroad was indeed over-generous with its resources—but it got its solid bed! The trains ran.

So it is with the love of Jesus. Only, in the case of Jesus, the love is so much greater than it need be that any comparison with any human endeavor makes the human action pale by contrast. Truly, the love of Jesus is a generous love.

But this is characteristic of all God's dealings with his creation. God, at all times and at all places, has poured out himself to men in such lavish grace that it seems incredible, yet in Jesus it is no sacrilege to say that he "went the second mile" —the mile to Calvary. Truly, the love of Jesus is a generous love.

But the love of Jesus is also a gentle love.

The Scripture says of him: "He shall not strive, nor cry; neither shall any man hear his voice in the streets. A bruised reed shall he not break, and smoking flax shall he not quench, till he send forth judgment unto victory. And in his name shall the Gentiles trust (Matt. 12:19–21)."

Human beings can be gentle and loving. Some years ago, in Waxahachie, Texas, the hearts of many people were touched by the plight of a little nine-month-old child.[2] The baby had been born without arms. Her callous parents abandoned her. When people found out about the case, many offered to adopt her, and a fund of $3,000 was swiftly subscribed for her benefit. While authorities were trying to decide what to do with the child, a middle-aged Dallas couple, people of more than moderate means and motivated by religious reasons—they had Jesus in their hearts—came forward and adopted the baby, not for glory or renown (for they asked that their names not be revealed), but solely out of the kind of love that would make one want to put one's arms around an armless child. A gentle love. Like the gentle love of the personal Jesus.

Human beings can have gentle imaginations. The final scene of the film *All Quiet on the Western Front*—the first version, silent, and black and white, made years ago—shows this painfully. The young German soldier is in the trenches on a day very close to the end of World War I. Shortly before, his best friend has been killed. All around him is the mud and the desolation, the destruction and despair of war. Yet in this nightmare world a single beautiful butterfly floats gently by and alights on a sandbag at the trench's edge. The young German soldier is hardly more than a schoolboy himself. With a child's innocence he leaves the protection of the trench and reaches for the butterfly. A French sniper's bullet kills him—but he has died reaching for beauty. With one gentle gesture he dies. And all is quiet on the Western Front.

Of course, the stories we remember about human beings are ordinarily not the gentle ones. It is said of the gangster from the Prohibition Era, Dutch Schultz, that the final gesture of his life was faithful to the kind of man he was. All his misspent, criminal life Schultz had been able to bribe his way out of almost any kind of difficulty. Crudely. Obviously. There was nothing "gentle" about the gangster, Dutch Schultz. So the day he was shot, the last day of his life, when the ambulance got him to the hospital, from the stretcher on which they were carrying him, he reached into his pocket and handed the intern who bent over him a roll of bills. "Here's something for you, pal," he said. "Take good care of me." There was $725 in the roll of bills, but it did not do Dutch Schultz a bit of good.[3] He died.

Probably many persons would say that the attitude of the

gangster is the most representative of human beings, that we are not normally gentle. I wonder. I wonder if the difference doesn't lie in a man's relationship to Christ. Yes, a Chicago gangster may be brutal and cynical and far from gentle—but he's not a Christian. A middle-aged Dallas couple, two Christian human beings who will put their arms around an abandoned armless child—is not this more normal?

Still, for all the examples of man's gentleness to man, nothing can compare with the gentleness of the love of Jesus. The Scripture accounts thrill us. Ah, how marvelous it must have been to walk those Judean hills with Jesus, my Lord! How wonderful it must have been to have heard his gentle voice! How precious must have been the sight of his face! How thrilling it must have been to watch him heal the sick and comfort the afflicted!

The Lord has blessed me in my years in the ministry. Ah, how he has blessed me! I will always be grateful to him for calling me into his wonderful service, for giving me the opportunity to serve him. And I have known from the beginning of my ministry what a blessing the ministry is. But, like most pastors, it is only after years in the ministry that I can appreciate fully all the blessings. Sorrow. Tragedy. Affliction. Across the years I have shared Jesus with many in the church family, ministering in time of sorrow, tragedy, affliction. Like all pastors—and all Christians—I have helped bear other's burdens. Early in a man's ministry it is difficult to understand how such sharing can be a blessing—but blessing it is. I suppose it is because, in comforting others by pointing them to the gentle love of the personal Jesus, one is reinforced time and again by contact with that same gentle Jesus. The love of Jesus is gentle.

But it is also joyous.

It is joyous because it is supposed to be joyous. Joy is the normal condition of the Christian. Jesus said, "I am come that they might have life, and that they might have it more abundantly (John 10:10)." It is interesting to note that the "more abundantly" used here does not mean mere quantity, but quality; it is not merely a whole lot more of the same old thing, but a quality of life lived above the common.

But a life lived above the common is normal for the Christian, and a life filled with joy is normal for the Christian, for the love of Jesus is a joyous love. A children's book of a few years ago has an amusing title: *The Way Things 'Spozed to Be.* This is the way life is supposed to be for the Christian—joyous.

My friend Bill Cannon shares the following from his family. When Bill was in seminary, one day he took his youngest daughter, Claire, into one of the large drugstores we have here in Fort Worth. At the cosmetic counter there was one of these factory representative "demonstrators" present to promote her firm's products. You know the type: the kind that looks as though she were pressed out of plastic, liquefied with lacquer, and bleached with brass. She leaned over the counter, smiled down at Bill's five-year-old daughter, and enquired archly: "And, my little girl, what do you want to be when you grow up?"

Well, most little girls want to be movie stars—or whatever else happens to be the "glamour" occupation of the day. And, given the "glamorous" look of the lacquered lady, what would you expect? Bill's daughter looked up at her with understandable awe. And Bill's daughter was—and is—quite pretty.

"Tell me," the woman coaxed, "what do you want to be when you grow up?"

"I want to be a housewife," Bill's daughter said.

A housewife. Nothing fake or phony. Nothing lacquered or lying. Nothing plastic or pretending. But an honest-to-goodness, real, genuine, Christian housewife.

And a housewife—a happy, joyous, Christian housewife—she became, because that is what she felt she was supposed to be, not because she lacked the talent to do anything else (Claire is talented; at one time she even wrote a column for

*Tell* magazine), but because she knows that you are happiest doing what you are supposed to do.

God did not intend for us not to be followers of Jesus. We are supposed to be children of God. We are supposed to follow the Lord. It is normal to be a saved, born again, child of the King. And there is happiness and joy in doing what comes naturally.

Remember Mrs. McArthur, the lady with whom we began this chapter? She experienced the generous, gentle, joyous love of my personal Jesus in February; my brother pastor tells me that the flowers in the garden around her house were never lovelier than in the spring and summer following.

If your life is mean and drab, if your days are dark and murky, let the love of Jesus come into your heart; let your life bloom for Jesus.

And if Jesus is already in your heart, if you already know the love of the personal Jesus, then share that love. I used as a text for this chapter a verse dealing with the Forerunner, with John the Baptist, rather than with our Lord. "And thou shalt have joy and gladness; and many shall rejoice in his birth." This word to Zacharias can be legitimately extended to you, to anyone who shares in the sharing of the gospel. There is joy and gladness in witnessing to the love of the personal Jesus—joy and gladness, for many to whom you witness will rejoice in the birth, not of John the Baptist, but of Jesus, the personal Jesus.

A love that is generous, gentle, joyous—that is the love of the personal Jesus.

In the words of the old hymn:

> I will sing of my Redeemer
> And His wondrous love to me;
> On the cruel cross He suffered
> From the curse to set me free.
>
> I will tell the wondrous story,
> How my estate to save,

In his boundless love and mercy,
He the ransom freely gave.

I will praise my dear Redeemer,
His triumphant power I'll tell,
How the victory He giveth
Over sin and death and hell.

I will sing of my Redeemer,
And His heavenly love to me;
He from death to life hath brought me,
Son of God, with Him to be.

## NOTES

1. Robert G. Lee, *Sourcebook of 500 Illustrations* (Grand Rapids: Zondervan Publishing House, 1964), p. 81.
2. *Ibid.*, p. 71.
3. *Ibid.*, p. 87.

*And I, if I be lifted up from the earth, will draw all men unto me.* (John 12:32)

# 18 The Person of Jesus

Wisdom does not always come only with advancing years. Sometimes the young person will be led to display an insight far beyond his own calendar chronology. That is, if he knows the Person of Jesus Christ.

A brand-new convert, a teen-ager, a member of the erstwhile "Jesus Revolution," was appearing on a public panel with several other young people and with several preachers of the city. He was an earnest young man. He desired to witness for his Lord. He was doing a good job of it. But he lacked training, knowledge, and experience. So he was not prepared to deal with some of the questions that came from the audience. One adult in particular had apparently taken an extreme dislike for the young man and for everything the young man stood for. (That is, what the adult was trying to make the young man say he stood for. The young man had never thought it all out. He really did not know what he stood for—past a certain point.) The young man was getting the worst of it. In his attempts to answer the cutting questions thrown at him he was getting more and more confused. Suddenly, in mid-sentence, he stopped. He stood for a moment, completely still. As though listening. As though in silent prayer. A change came over his face. The confusion cleared away. The anxiety. In some strange way the boy seemed temporarily to mature. When he spoke, his voice was calm and confident, and his eyes were clear. He looked directly at the man who had harried him with questions, and this is in essence what he said:

"I don't know how to answer all the questions you ask me. Maybe when I get older, I will. But right now, all I know is that, if I keep my eyes on Jesus, keep walking toward him, all these other things will fall into place."

And of course they will, not only for that young man, but for all who call upon the Person of Jesus. That Person is the one true Guide; he who is God's Gift will bring us all to glory.

He is the true Guide; there are many false guides in this world because there are many false values. To hold a worthless value is to follow a false guide.

It is said that, in the closing days of the Civil War, after President Jefferson Davis had fled from Richmond, Virginia, Union soldiers overtook a convoy at the edge of the mountains outside Richmond and captured three wagons loaded with Confederate paper money. By face value there were literally fortunes in the wagons for the printed bills of currency were piled in the wagon beds like bales of cotton. Fortunes. But at face value only. The Union soldiers who guarded the captured convoy that night had run out of food; with all the millions at their fingertips there was no place they could buy food; and even if they had been transported to a modern supermarket, the money would have been useless.

(We laughingly say today that we should save our Confederate money; the South will rise again. At least this is good for a laugh. But there are other things of no value in the world that are not good for anything. The promises of the devil are completely without value; nothing will rise from any of his promises.)

The only true guide is Jesus. Sometimes old habits, old ways of thinking, old prejudices keep us as blinded from him as though we had bandaged our eyes. We act in ways that, in the secular world, might be considered eccentric. For example, there was an Englishman named Walter Lavender who liked horses and hated automobiles.[1] (There are times on our freeways when I think I know how he felt.) Mr. Lavender lived a full eighty-five years and obstinately refused to accept the fact that the automobile had replaced the horse. He once pointed to a motor hearse and told his family: "I don't want to go to my grave in one of them. It isn't fit and proper." On his deathbed he made his family promise that they would secure a horse-drawn hearse for his funeral. He died. The family discovered that there was not an undertaker in England who used horses. But Walter Lavender still got his desire; he was carried to his grave in a black carriage pulled by four bay horses, an equipage rented from a motion picture studio.

True, Mr. Lavender's old way of thinking got him his wish—but it guided him to the grave rather than to life.

Jesus is God's gift to the world of sinful men. "For God so loved the world, that he gave his only begotten Son, that whosoever believeth in him should not perish, but have everlasting life. (John 3:16)."

Human beings are capable of rich gifts. It is said that a concert violinist, Benno Rabinoff, accepted the invitation of a violin fan who arrived at the restaurant carrying a violin case which he opened after dinner. Inside was a genuine Stradivarius violin made in 1734, what experts would consider one of the three greatest violins in the world. It had once been owned by Fritz Kreisler and had been played by Kreisler in concert at Carnegie Hall. The violin fan gave it to Rabinoff there in the restaurant. "Why are you giving this to me?" Rabinoff asked in astonishment. The donor said, "I want to hear it sing again. It has been silent too long."[2]

But the opposite is often true.

The great evangelist of the Nineteenth Century, Dwight L. Moody, was fond of telling the following story. A steamboat (the river steamboats were the jet planes of their day) had stranded on a sand bar in the Mississippi River. The captain could not get the boat free. A tough-looking man came aboard and addressed the captain:

"I am told that you are in need of a pilot to help you out of this difficulty."

The captain answered: "Yes, we are. Are you a pilot?"

"Well, that's what they call me," answered the man.

"Do you know where the snags and sandbars are?"

"No, sir."

"Then how do you expect to run this steamboat if you do not know where the snags and the sandbars are? How do you expect to be of any help if you are not familiar with the places of danger?"

"Easy enough," the tough-looking man answered with confidence, "I know where they ain't."[3]

And that's the trouble with a lot of persons today; they know too many of the things that are not the gifts of God; they know him, the devil, who "ain't" instead of Him, the Christ, who is.

But Christ is a gift who cost God much; it cost him the death of his Son. There is cost in this gift even in the modern day.

Joseph B. Underwood, in his thrilling stories from the mission fields that show the power of the gospel in people's lives, tells the following story.

The attitude of a young African man illustrates the dedication necessary if this world is to be redeemed. Missionary Carlos Owens tells of the conversion of this young man in East Africa. When he abandoned the Muslim religion, his wife and five children abandoned him, unwilling to live with a man who turned from Islam to Christianity. In spite of his sorrow he continued to serve the Lord faithfully, growing in grace and knowledge of Jesus Christ. Some months later he felt that God was calling him to preach. In dedication to this task he prepared himself educationally and spiritually.

Carlos Owens helped him to prepare his first sermon, but when Sunday morning came the young man did not appear. After the worship service the missionary went to the home and found it empty. The next day the African appeared at the home of the missionary, his body broken and bleeding and horribly bruised. He told the missionary that on Saturday his brothers had come to his house determined that he was not to preach the gospel. They carried him into the woods. They beat his body and left him tied to the trees. Finally he managed to struggle free from his bonds. Wounded, bleeding, bruised, he staggered back a great distance to the home of the missionary.

As the missionary and his wife cleaned and dressed his wounds, the man looked up into their faces, his own face luminous with the joy of heaven as he exclaimed, "Even if they kill me I will still preach Christ!"[4]

The Person of Jesus is a gift for which many a man has died. But the Person of Jesus is also a glory, not only in Him alone, but often in the man who follows Jesus.

There is a poignant sidelight to this in the book *The Jesus Revolution: New Inspiration for Evangelicals* by William S. Cannon. The book is talking about a typical young person (typical, that is, of some of the young rebels—not of the majority of our fine young people, let me add) who had strayed from God's commands and home training, gone into the far country of the counter-culture, but finally reached for the Lord Jesus. The book describes the moment in these words:

> . . . So he met Christ—my Jesus and your Jesus, praise the Lord—and he was gloriously saved right there on the street, he became a member of God's forever family, and this time it was for real, man, for real. Glory, hallelujah, praise the Lord. Wow![5]

But the glory that we share on this earth is as nothing to the glory we will know when we meet our Lord in heaven. A Christian writer has said:

> One day, by a river, I found a deep-red stone, beautiful as agate. It had been cut by some action of nature, and was shaped like one-half of the human heart. I began to look for the other half, feeling sure that it must be somewhere, for in that piece of stone in my hand was evidence of the other part.

Years ago that was; but I have continued to look for, and dream that I should find, the other half of that heart-shaped stone—which lies before me as I write, eloquent in its appeal to me to seek always until I find its lost counterpart.[6]

One day, when we meet the Lord in heaven, you and I who are Christians, you and I who know the personal Jesus, you and I who know the glory of having been saved, will know what it is like to have our hearts reunited with God's heart. But until that day, the advice of our young friend, the boy with whom I began this chapter, is still very good advice indeed. Keep your eyes upon Jesus! Keep your eyes upon Him!

Or, as the hymn writer put it:

The whole world was lost in the darkness of sin,
The Light of the world is Jesus;
Like sunshine at noonday His glory shone in,
The Light of the world is Jesus.

No darkness have we who in Jesus abide,
The Light of the world is Jesus;
We walk in the light when we follow our guide,
The Light of the world is Jesus.

Ye dwellers in darkness with sin-blinded eyes,
The Light of the world is Jesus;
Go, wash at His bidding, and light will arise,
The Light of the world is Jesus.

No need of the sunlight in heaven we're told,
The Light of the world is Jesus;
The Lamb is the Light in the city of gold,
The Light of the world is Jesus.

Jesus, the Personal Jesus. Is he your Jesus? Do you know him as a Person? Does he live in your heart? I would, my friend, that he did. And, if he does not, I offer to you my Personal Jesus; I pray that you will open your heart to him.

## NOTES

1. Lee, *op. cit.*, pp. 151–152.
2. *Ibid.*, pp. 135–136.
3. *Ibid.*, pp. 151–152.
4. Joseph B. Underwood, *By Love Compelled* (Nashville: Broadman Press, 1966), pp. 118-119.
5. William S. Cannon, *The Jesus Revolution: New Inspiration for Evangelicals* (Nashville: Broadman Press, 1971), p.33.
6. Gordon Hurlbutt, compiler, *Wings of the Spirit* (Louisville: The Standard Press, 1928), p. 349.